The Secret of Successful Acquisitions

T0345923

Dr. Farsam Farschtschian is an Investment Advisor at Morgan Stanley in London, covering German speaking Europe. He holds a PhD degree in Business Administration from the University of St. Gallen and is a Research Associate at its IFPM Centre of Corporate Governance. Farsam Farschtschian first wrote about his empirical findings in his thesis *The Role of Boards in Directing and Controlling Acquisitions* in 2010. Previously, he studied at the Universities of Geneva and Berkeley and holds a Master's degree in Political Science with a focus on International Relations.

Farsam Farschtschian

The Secret of Successful Acquisitions

Abandoning the Myth of Board Influence

Campus Verlag
Frankfurt/New York

ISBN 978-3-593-39438-1

Copyright © 2011 Campus Verlag GmbH, Frankfurt am Main
Umschlaggestaltung: Guido Klütsch, Köln
Satz: Fotosatz L. Huhn, Linsengericht
Druck und Bindung: Beltz Druckpartner, Hemsbach
Gedruckt auf Papier aus zertifizierten Rohstoffen (FSC/PEFC).
Printed in Germany

For my parents

Contents

German preface for editionMALIK

Die alte Welt vergeht,
weil eine neue Welt entsteht.

Wirtschaft und Gesellschaft gehen durch eine der tiefgreifendsten Umwandlungen, die es geschichtlich je gab. Als Begriff wählte ich 1997 dafür »Die Große Transformation«, denn bereits damals war das Ausmaß des heraufziehenden epochalen Wandels deutlich zu sehen. Was heute lediglich als eine finanzielle und ökonomische Krise zu eng gesehen wird, kann weit besser als die Geburtswehen der neuen Welt des 21. Jahrhunderts verstanden werden.

In dieser neuen Welt werden Organisationen eine höhere Ebene des Funktionierens erreichen. Sie werden doppelt so gut wie bisher funktionieren, aber nur die Hälfte des Geldes dafür benötigen. Die universelle Herausforderung wird für sie das Meistern von bisher noch nie erfahrener Komplexität durch neues Management sein.

Geld ist dafür aber weit weniger wichtig als Intelligenz, Vorstellungskraft, Information, Kommunikation und Gestaltungswille. Das neue Wissen hierfür und darauf gestützt neue, biokybernetische Lösungen sind bereits da. Deren Kern sind die °Evolutionären Naturgesetze aus Kybernetik und Bionik für das Selbstorganisieren und Selbstregulieren. Diese Gesetze zu verstehen und sie zu nutzen ist das neue Kapital der neuen Welt und die Grundlage für Leadership von Personen und Organisationen.

Die editionMALIK ist die Plattform für das zuverlässige Funktionieren von Organisationen in der hochkomplexen Umwelt des 21. Jahrhunderts. Sie ist die systemische Orientierungs- und Navigationshilfe für Leader, die den Wandel vorausdenken und -lenken.

Fredmund Malik
St. Gallen, Januar 2010

Über Malik sagt der Doyen des Managements, Peter F. Drucker:

> »Fredmund Malik has become the leading analyst of, and expert on, management in Europe as it has emerged in the last thirty years – and a powerful force in shaping it … . He is a commanding figure – in theory as well as in the practice of management.«

Preface by Helmut Maucher

Farsam Farschtschian's analysis of M&A and the board of directors' evolving responsibilities addresses the subject in a way that has never been done before.

Studies of M&A typically only take strategy, objectives and the related roles and actions into account. To date, these studies have not considered the way in which the board and management cooperate on these questions or the division of their roles and responsibilities. He illustrates, in a very striking way, the difference between the way in which legislation views these roles and the reality, and what should, practically, be done. In this way, Farsam Farschtschian has identified a crucial gap in current research.

Mr. Farschtschian's analysis demonstrates that today's business world is becoming progressively more diverse, there are not only clear so-called traditional acquisitions, but new diverse forms are emerging in the shape of co-operations, joint ventures, alliances, participations and so on. This, in turn, implies new forms of corporate governance and organisational structures, which he argues require, to a certain extent, different qualities in top managers. He also explores the elements of a productive leadership environment created though board-management interactions, which differ according to the firm's structure and the quality and philosophy of the CEO.

I believe that this analysis is, in many ways, highly original. Farsam Farschtschian's work is greatly enriched by the detailed depiction of the reality of top management's work in the context of M&A and by the exploration of how experienced business leaders think about these matters and have dealt with them.

This book deserves a broad readership and I hope that many managers dealing with such matters benefit from this research.

Dr. h.c. Helmut Maucher
Honorary Chairman of Nestlé

Acknowledgements

First and foremost, I would like to thank Prof. Dr. Martin Hilb and Prof. Dr. Fredmund Malik at the University of St. Gallen. Their contribution to my understanding of the board room was critical to my work.

It is not matter of course that internationally renowned business leaders who shaped some of today's most successful multinational companies showed interest and committed their time and knowledge to this book. In particular, I would like to thank Dr. h.c. Helmut Maucher. He made this work possible, practical and, most importantly, relevant in the context of the changing face of leadership and corporate governance in the 21st century. Many of his ideas on leadership informed the conclusions of this work.

I am also very grateful to board directors who gave me access to unique company sources that are selectively incorporated in this book. I would especially like to acknowledge the contributions of Philippe de Weck, Bruno de Kalbermatten and Dr. h.c. Fritz Gerber. In addition, Dr. h.c. Thomas Thomas Schmidheiny's valuable insights, along with contributions from other senior executives, lawyers and academics enriched my research markedly.

I would like to thank Ms. Deirdre Mullins. Her contribution was beyond editorial, and her critical questioning of my arguments made her an indispensable resource.

Finally, I would like to thank my team and colleagues at Morgan Stanley. Their support along with many discussions over the last couple of years was vital to completing this book alongside my daily professional duties.

Dr. Farsam Farschtschian
London, 2011

1. From Abandoning the Myth to the Required »Leadership Environment«

1.1 Abandoning the Myth

Acquisitions are one of the most important business activities that a company conducts: they represent the most visible part of firm strategies, and as a complex phenomenon, they are proof of companies' capabilities and ultimately of leadership. At the same time, they are one of the most risky strategic manoeuvres. Despite the fact that acquisition success factors are known, the majority of acquisitions still fail. Surprisingly, there are still no adequate theories to explain this phenomenon, despite the tremendously negative impact of these failures and the vast amount of academic and practical research on M&A.

Some supporting *structural management elements* must be lacking therefore. Either the board or the management body must not be functioning properly, and hence their interaction is not optimised. In other words, the *»leadership environment«*, in terms of the company's orientation, TMT structure, power relations and interaction, is not facilitating successful acquisition. In order to change this, the vital question, therefore, is *»Who is responsible for creating this environment«?*

Prima facie, the board of directors.

Backed by academic research illustrating the board of directors as the highest governing authority within the management structure with ultimate, overall responsibility for the management of the company's business, my analysis began by looking at the role of boards in acquisitions.

But as a result of many discussions with business leaders who have created some of today's leading multinational companies, I discovered that literature with regard to boards' roles was largely inadequate and *counterintuitively* boards were not, in practice, as significant to the acquisition process as initially presumed despite their status in the law and emphasis in corporate governance.

Indeed, considering the board's theoretical importance perhaps the most surprising thing about all of this is that the role of boards of directors in acquisition has barely been researched to date. Instead, most work concentrates on generating key acquisition success factors without concomitantly touching upon *the necessary leadership environment that enables effective implementation of these factors.*

1.2 Required »Leadership Environment«

As a result of this insight, my analysis shifted to the top management team (TMT) as a whole, which includes the board and the CEO with his team. This enables a holistic perspective of how acquisitions are run and should be run *as an extension of a constructive leadership environment.*

In order to identify the key conditions for this, I carried out extensive qualitative field work and analysed two specific case studies in depth. Peter Drucker, as a management thinker widely accepted and recognised by academics and foremost practitioners, established six principles for successful acquisition. These are used to analyse the way in which the board and the management interacted in their relative fulfilment of each of these six acquisition principles, which ultimately allowed to qualify the leadership environment.

In this way, this book aims to make a significant contribution to practice by striving to provide boards and managers with tools enabling them to perform more effectively within acquisitions, ultimately leading to higher acquisition success rates[1].

---

1   From a stock market perspective and building on my professional background, time and time again, history has clearly demonstrated that companies with good management, where management adopt a long-term approach, deliver superior returns to their shareholders. Nestle is an outstanding example of the beneficial impact that long-term strategic management can have on shareholder returns, delivering nearly 70% share price outperformance relative to world markets over the last 10 years. Despite the evidence, analysts and investors frequently ignore this factor when making investment decisions, instead preferring to rely on short-term valuation and earnings momentum factors. This is arguably a key reason why these decisions frequently prove to be wrong.

1.3 Two Polar Opposite Key Case Studies: an Introduction

In order to do this, two cases are explored in this book, *Nestlé* and *Swissair Group,* as polar opposite examples. Nestlé's acquisition strategy, under the leadership of its long-standing chairman and CEO, Helmut Maucher, was highly successful not only in terms of acquiring companies, but also in their integration into the whole organisation. In contrast, the Swissair Group experienced the most dramatic bankruptcy in Swiss economic history as a direct result of its acquisition strategy.

Despite the current trend and bias towards quantitative lead research, it would be a scientific and methodological miscomprehension to believe that empirical research has to consist of mainly numerical quantification. In order to analyse the complex human relationships involved in board-management interaction, the qualitative method is a more appropriate approach in terms of its explanatory power. Hence, I made an attempt in this book to identify which board-management relationships positively contribute to a leadership environment that enables good acquisition results with the goal of proposing best practices in acquisitions for boards of directors.

Moreover, as the case studies will reveal, *the reality is markedly different to the theory of corporate governance in terms of the board-management relationship.* This raises fundamental questions about whether current corporate governance adequately reflects the reality of today's business world and the current structural transformations resulting from new types of business practices and methods (this is the subject of the outlook chapter of this book).

2. The Key Facts of Corporate Governance

The Cadbury Report, which is a Code of Best Practice formally entitled »The Report of the Committee on the Financial Aspects of Corporate Governance«, published in December 1992, was the first report aiming to improve corporate governance. The committee defined corporate governance as »the system by which companies are directed and controlled«. The Report presents recommendations for the executive directors, non-executive directors, and those responsible for reporting and control.

Corporate governance aims to discover what constitutes fair regulation of the power balance between a company's board and management. While corporate governance defines the roles of boards and recommends ways to actively animate them, it does not analyse their role in the face of a decisive kind of event such as M&A. This gap in the literature is reflected in the codes of corporate governance where there is no provision for dealing with acquisitions.

While TMT in literature often relates to the chief executive and his management team, for the purpose of this book TMT includes both the executive management body of a company as well as the board of directors.

2.1 Introduction to Corporate Governance

To understand the duties of a board of directors, it is important to contextualise the emergence of the board of directors as a controlling body, in the broader corporate governance discussion.

The subject of corporate governance has been discussed in literature for a long time. Debate most likely began with the emergence of larger corporations in which, for the first time, ownership no longer coincided with management and disunion between the owners and managers in organisations led to a principal-agent situation (»agency theory«). In the late 18th century, control over resources was thus transferred from owners to managers.

Discussion of how to define management tasks and control by shareholders began. Monks & Minow (2001, p. 94) posit that this separation was first discussed by the authors Berle & Means (1932). Other authors even quote Smith (1776), who already discerned problems in the motivation of managers »of other people's money« to the extent that managers' interests do not align with the principals.

The term »corporate governance« has only been in use since the 1980s. The earlier discussions mainly came under the topic of »agency theory«, i.e., that the disunion between the owners and managers in organisations leads to a principal-agent situation.

When the focus of corporate governance is defined as directing the company in the interest of its shareholders and as controlling management's actions on their behalf, it is obvious that these two concepts refer to the same research area. Hart (1995) demonstrated the overlap when he explained that corporate governance issues are related to agency and transaction cost issues. As both of these exist in publicly traded companies, agency theory appears to be the basic framework for corporate governance structures.

2.2 An Agency Perspective

Many authors consider the focal point of corporate governance to be the agency relationship between owners and managers of a company. Looking back in history, most companies were directed by their owners until the late 18th to early 19th century. At some point, however, the amount of capital and managerial resources needed in large and expanding companies led to the sale of equity to the public. Due to the increased size of the companies, it became necessary to hire managers to lead a company on the owner's behalf. With this, the ownership and management of companies separated.

The classic principal-agent situation is characterised by the conflicts that may result due to the differing interests of owners and managers. This was already described in the early days of larger companies: Adam Smith pointed out in 1776 that managers do not have the same interest in promoting a firm's success as they would have if they owned the company (Smith 1776).

In agency theory, solutions to these problems are recommended in the form of efficient contracts that force the agent to behave according to the owner's intention. The perspective of Jensen & Meckling (1976), who describe a company as a nexus of contracts, is often used to describe the agency problem.

This theory needs expansion, however, since the principal-agent situation no longer exists. Instead, »the owner« is usually a diverse group of shareholders, and, in addition, other stakeholders often influence the relationship or even take on the role of yet another principal. Furthermore, structures have developed between the principal and agent in the form of intermediates, especially supervisory boards, which clearly do not represent just one of the parties.

The question of *whose interests the boards should serve* is therefore vital to understanding the purpose of a supervising body, as supervision and control can be exercised in quite different ways, depending on what goals are being pursued.

2.3 Whose Interests Are Served?

Building on the above, one immediate conclusion would be that supervision must be conducted in the interest of the owners, i.e., the shareholders. After all, supervision became necessary due to the separation of ownership and management. There are, however, two other possibilities: to manage a company in the interest of the stakeholders, amongst whom the shareholders may or may not be counted; or, one could assume that *the company, as a legal personality, has an interest in its own right* and should therefore be managed accordingly.

Aspects in favour of the owners' interests are the fact that, initially, the supervisory committee was created to represent the owners. This situation was certainly valid until the 19th century (Drucker 1994). It could also be argued that, from a legal perspective, the owners of a company have the right to conduct their company's business the way they like. After all, anyone can do whatever he wants with his own property, as long as it conforms to the law.

Another question now arises: *what interests of the owners should be pursued?* As soon as there is more than one owner, one is potentially confronted with diverging interests.

This is best seen in large corporations, which can be owned by thousands of shareholders. Some of these shareholders may have bought the shares hoping that the stock price would skyrocket in the short run (e.g., this often occurs in situations of M&A speculation) and they would be able to make a fast profit. Others may regard their shares as a long-term investment, count on the payout of dividends or may even wish to pass them on to their children. Furthermore, some people may have emotional reasons for taking a stake in a company. In the most extreme case there are as many interests as shareholders. On which of these interests should the supervising body's actions now be based? Depending on this, the perception of a board's duties varies completely.

It should also be mentioned that this question cannot be answered in a democratic way: stating that the interest of the majority is all-dominant would mean that, in the long run, nobody would buy shares anymore. Becoming a minority shareholder would mean that the majority could do whatever it likes with one's money and the minority shareholder could not count on his interests being considered effectively. This would imply that a public company could no longer do what it is there for, i.e., raising capital in order to act with this capital according to its purpose.

In this context, there is the view that at least one interest is shared by all owners, which is the maximization of return on capital of every single shareholder. The management should be bound to this goal. This so-called *shareholder value approach* was designed by Alfred Rappaport (1998).

As ultimate ownership of a company resides with the shareholders, many practitioners and researchers argue for a shareholder value perspective. Some authors argue that shareholders are the most vulnerable stakeholders, since all others can ensure their position by efficient contracting with the firm (Williamson 1984, 1985). In contrast, others argue that focusing on only one principal lowers the cost of decision-making and restricts managerial discretion.

The authors Jensen & Meckling (1976) add the reasoning of economical efficiency to this view. They assume the existence of complete contracts with all other stakeholders, thereby leaving all residual claims with the shareholders, and assume therefore that agency problems would not exist. Since these assumptions do not hold – especially due to managerial agency problems – a pure shareholder view could lead to inefficient investments; excess risk-taking in highly-levered firms might occur, as well as underinvestment in the case of debt overhang.

In this case, a shareholder plus debt provider perspective would seem to be economically efficient (Shleifer & Vishny 1997). It has become obvious, however, that numerous companies that were managed according to this concept have recently experienced substantial difficulties.

In order for corporations to be governed efficiently in their entirety, some argue for the employment of a broader *stakeholder perspective*. It is important to note the greater importance of stakeholders other than finance providers in Continental Europe.

Many proponents of the shareholder value theory thereupon switched to the stakeholder approach, which was developed in 1952 by the past chairman and CEO of General Electric, Ralph Cordiner (Malik 2003, p. 37). This approach was abandoned later. According to the stakeholder approach, the centre of focus is the interests of the employees, suppliers and investors. Depending on the interpretation, shareholders could also be regarded as stakeholders.

Some researchers and journalists argue that there is no substantial difference between shareholder and stakeholder value as a consideration of important stakeholders is part of achieving a sustainable shareholder value. The key term in the discussion is »*sustainable*«. In theory, assuming that the markets correctly evaluate the future cash flows of companies, including long-term aspects, there is no reason to call a shareholder value orientation short-term. But since the assumption of perfect markets does not hold, a strategy focusing on short-term stock price performance at the stock market is possible.

The stakeholder value orientation demands a stronger orientation towards serving all stakeholders and thereby laying the foundation for sustainable development. It is argued by many Europeans that American shareholder value orientation considers other stakeholders too insignificant for sustainable economic development, and therefore also for sustainable shareholder value.

2.4　A Third Approach

Both the shareholder and the stakeholder approach have a shared focus on interest groups. An alternative approach would be to *regard the interest of the company itself as central*. One of the first proponents of this theory was Peter Drucker who is considered to be the father of modern management. According to him, the separation of management and supervision alone expresses the idea that the company cannot and must not be managed in the interest of a specific group (Drucker 1993).

In line with Drucker's view, Malik (2002, p. 30) suggests that one should act on the assumption that the company has an interest of its own:

»Instead of focusing on the interests of the diverse interest groups (...) I suggest, that the company itself is regarded as a productive unit that creates standard of living and wealth the more effectively, the better it functions, and as such completely independent of any specific interests of the various interest groups.« (Fredmund Malik)

According to Malik, this approach offers the best guarantee that management will align itself with the prosperity of an organisation. He further states that if a company is conducted in the interests of the various interest groups, an organisation becomes a playing field of changing political and social powers which can potentially lead to the destabilization of the entire company. Malik (2002) argues, therefore, against both shareholder and stakeholder approaches.

Malik (2005) calls for the »strength« of the company as the top priority of corporate governance, and not interest groups, such as shareholders or stakeholders:

»Corporate capitalism, not stakeholder or shareholder capitalism. Ask the question – what is a strong company – what is a strong, viable company? The answer is: a company that has happy customers.« (Fredmund Malik)

Malik explains a *corporation's purpose as that of »creating customers«* and if a corporation has customers it will, as a consequence, have happy shareholders. Instead of shareholder value or stakeholder value, he coins *»customer value«* as the guiding principle for entrepreneurially led companies.

With regard to the purpose of a company, Peter Drucker initially speaks about »economic performance« of the company and then states that »there is only one valid definition of business purpose: to create a customer« (1993, p. 35). Malik shares this opinion and adds that customers must be satisfied with the company's services and products in order to *remain* customers. He further notes that customers are satisfied if, and only if, the company supplies them with more benefit than other competitors in the market. This implies that a company has to be competitive (Malik, 2003, p. 36). *Competitiveness*, therefore, can also be understood as part of the definition of purpose, and is related to Drucker's expression of »economic performance«.

This logic ultimately leads to the idea that the organisation's interest cannot be confused with that of the management. Furthermore, a company that has customers has the greatest opportunity to fulfil the interests of all

groups, they »will always find investors and, ultimately, will also have satisfied shareholders and stakeholders, not as an objective, but as a consequence
of successful management« (Malik 2002, p. 36).

All of these approaches have their merits and consequences. I believe
there are many good arguments in favour of placing the management under
the service of the interest of the company itself and in this book this approach is used. It is important to stress, however, that this analysis explores
only one choice among several possibilities.

There is an ongoing debate as to whose interest the CEO should serve.
In practice, however, I note that CEOs usually follow the wishes of those
principals with the greatest power over their future. This is typically the
majority shareholders, who elect the directors, who then support or dismiss
the CEO.

2.5 Boards of Directors Come into Play

Despite a more stakeholder-oriented perspective in Continental Europe,
there is still a need to fulfil the interests of the many principals rather
than those of managers. But there is a collective action problem (especially
among shareholders), as costs of intervention have to be borne by the acting
individual(s), while the benefits are mostly shared by all shareholders.

Boards of directors were created to overcome this issue. Indeed, the law
and corporate governance regulations require such a body in companies,
that shares the interests of the shareholders and to which the CEO is responsible.

It should be mentioned, however, that the establishment of a board of
directors cannot directly solve the agency problem. Instead, the problem is
split into two parts: an agency problem *between shareholders and the board,*
and another *between the board and management.* This begs the question:
who monitors the monitors? The structure is prescribed in many countries
in one form or another and it appears to be seen as a positive structure;
however, the discussion about its optimal design remains a central topic in
the corporate governance debate.

Discussion of board models revolves around the question of how and
in what structures boards can be used to overcome the common agency
problem between top management and shareholders or more stakeholders.
Because boards are required by law for all large companies in industrialized

nations and legislators put such strong emphasis on them, it is useful to discuss their role and the way in which they function.

2.5.1 Boards' Current Position and Challenges

Current corporate governance developments mean that boards, as the governing body of the firm, have become sensitised to their responsibilities and more dutiful in critically analysing and approving management proposals, such as acquisitions and other strategical business matters. However, directors on the board are confronted with a *double-edged sword* with regard to their involvement in corporate strategy:

On the one hand, there are significant external pressures for a *strong involvement* in important strategic corporate decisions (see the debates on corporate governance, investor activism, legal threats, etc.). Furthermore, the involvement of boards is not only externally motivated in terms of better control, but it is an increasingly accepted opinion among academics and practitioners that board directors, with their knowledge and experience, are an instrumental resource to firms which they should utilise.

On the other hand, in order for boards of directors to maintain their *independence,* a key quality of directors as described by the literature, boards are expected not to overly involve themselves in daily operational activities of a company. If boards interfere too much in the firm's management, they may alienate the top management team, and particularly the chief executive of the firm. It should also be noted, that even if boards would like to interfere more frequently, directors generally do not have sufficient time to do so, nor, very often, the specific knowledge to be more involved in daily operational corporate activities.

Therefore, boards of directors have a challenging and difficult task. The contrast in these prescribed roles in terms of *support* and *control* is concerning for boards. Boards have a fiduciary responsibility to the company's owners to act in the interest of the owner's investments; however, directors must fulfil this responsibility in a manner that does not alienate management's responsibility for running the business (Lorsch & MacIver 1989). Nevertheless, boards of directors remain, in the eyes of the law, the most important body of a firm, due to their ultimate responsibility and accountability for it.

Corporate acquisitions, for example, illustrate the most complex matters firms face. Bearing in mind that many boards of directors serve only on a part-time basis and because they often have no executive experience within the corporation, they lack both specific information and time to deal suitably with the given complexities.

Furthermore, boards lack guidance. Surprisingly, there is barely any discussion of best practices by academics, practitioners and consultants that could be of assistance to directors in performing their roles (Oliver 2000, p. 8).

2.5.2 Discussion of Individual Board Characteristics

Most board models discuss board structures, composition, remuneration or processes. Only some of them try to integrate these issues (Hilb 2002). Various aspects of board characteristics are described in this section.

Board Structure

There are many kinds of board structures. The biggest difference between these various forms is that some boards have *a one-tier* and others *a two-tier structure.*

One-tier boards combine shareholder representatives and the top management team on one board. The board, therefore, fulfils the roles of adviser, decision maker and monitor as one group. Since conflicts of interest are sure to evolve between these functions, committees are set up to focus on certain functions, e.g., executive committees for decision-making (or at least for decision preparation), advisory committees for specific aspects such as technological specialties, compensation committees, and audit committees. Nevertheless, within the entire board these functions overlap although it is sometimes difficult, or even impossible, to fulfil two tasks at the same time.

The main advantage of the one-tier board is the opportunity it gives of having shareholder representatives, independent outsiders and the TMT on one board, which can improve communication between them. It also allows, in principle, the combination of the roles of CEO and chairman. This can ease decision-making and creates the possibility of having one person responsible at the top of the company rather than two. Although such a concentration of power in one person is often criticised as resulting in too little board control, it can be helpful for fast decision-making.

Overall, I believe too much attention is given to this matter in the current corporate governance discussion. As I will explain in chapter 6, it is by far more important that companies have a solid successorship plan in place for the chief executive. As such, should the board of directors not be satisfied by the performance of its CEO at any point in time, an appropriate leader ought to be available as a competent, strong and, importantly, tested alternative to run the business. This is more significant than the debate contesting the union of the chief executive and the chairman function. To date it has still not received the attention it deserves. As conversations with leading CEOs have demonstrated, I believe that the decision to have a combined CEO-chairman position is situational and should be decided solely by the company itself.

The literature, however, describes various disadvantages associated with CEO duality. Based on the agency theory, CEO duality is associated with a much lower monitoring efficiency since, in his or her simultaneous function as chairperson, the CEO can effectively control the board by, for example, setting the board agenda or influencing the succession of directors and executives (Pearce & Zahra 1992). CEO duality may thus lead to a lack of checks and balances. Furthermore, when combining the two positions, firms may also have lower information processing capabilities, particularly in complex issues such as international business, which is why international companies are likely to separate the two jobs (Sanders & Carpenter 1998). While there is limited empirical support for the superiority of separated leadership structures (Dalton et al 1998), there seems to be agreement that CEO duality should be avoided.

In contrast, *two-tier boards* separate board functions more strictly. While the management board is committed to running the business and to preparing strategic decisions, the supervisory board focuses on approving or denying such proposals, on monitoring management, and on the hire, dismissal and compensation of the TMT. This allows for a greater focus on tasks with less conflict of interests. It does, however, put the supervisory directors in a less strategic role with potentially less communication with the TMT.

Although these two board structures are superficially very different, they work in very similar ways: the appointment of committees in the one-tier system substitutes the task division of the two-tier structure, shareholder representatives often have a speaker or even appoint the chairman of one-tier boards, supervisory boards engage in direct discussions with management, and meeting frequency has always been similar in both structures. Furthermore, both structures have developed towards having four to five committees, in particular for auditing and remuneration.

These days, the audit committee is crucial. Large companies have become increasingly complex and committee members are required to take on even more responsibility. For this reason, authors call not only for educated directors but also for their strong personal commitment (Bender & Vater 2004).

In the past, many companies had an executive committee that was used as a substitute for the full board when immediate actions were required or as a preparatory body for proposals prior to disclosure to the full board (Kesner 1988). The rising number of committees shows that much of the board's work is actually done by board committees.

Establishing special board committees has several advantages. Committees break down task complexity for directors (Kesner 1988, Bilimoria & Piderit 1994) and through the division of labour, each task can be handled in much more detail and directors are able to become experts in their assigned tasks. The smaller group size also allows for better group dynamics with less coordination costs. Lastly, committees allow for certain functions (such as deciding on remuneration) to be performed by independent outside members only.

Nevertheless, there are clearly also arguments against committees. Foremost, there are concerns that committees create two classes of directors, despite the board members being equally responsible. Furthermore, specialist directors on the committees may not have all the relevant information on the issues facing the firm. Empirical research on the performance impact of board committees is still limited. Klein (1998) found that, overall, board composition is unrelated to firm performance but that the percentage of inside directors on finance and accounting committees positively impacts firm performance. Thus, on the whole, committees are considered beneficial to a board in fulfilling its control role.

Board Composition

Board composition has been the focus of a great deal of research, albeit with contradictory findings. Important elements of composition are board size, insider-outsider ratio, diversity, and interlocks.

Among the most analysed variables is *board size*. Large boards are associated with both advantages and disadvantages (Dalton, Daily, Johnson & Ellstrand 1999). The advantages of large boards are mostly based on arguments from the resource dependency perspective. Having more directors increases the number of links with the external environment. Large boards are also favoured in light of the stewardship perspective, since a larger board can draw upon a larger pool of expertise and experience, as well as possessing higher cognitive processing capabilities. There are, however, significant disadvantages associated with large boards. From an agency theory perspective, larger boards tend to be ineffective monitors because individual directors can hide behind the mass.

Large boards may also complicate decision-making processes. While empirical evidence is ambiguous (Dalton et al. 1999), medium-sized boards appear ideal, as they benefit from a significant pool of expertise and external links, while not suffering from excessive coordination and communication costs.

Furthermore, according to the agency perspective, *board independence* is considered a crucial characteristic. While there are varying attempts to measure independence objectively, most research uses the inside-outside board member ratio as a proxy. A large number of outsiders is seen as advantageous for boards with regard to fulfilment of their monitoring role. Inside directors' careers are directly linked to the chief executive. They could therefore be cautious in objecting to the CEO's projects. However, a large number of outsiders can also bring disadvantages.

Unlike full-time officers of the firm, the part-time outside members typically know less about the organisation's businesses (Carpenter 2001). Moreover, outside directors may divide their resources between several other organisations or positions. This limits the board's involvement and contribution to all three roles of service, strategy, and control. While intuitively appealing, there is limited empirical support for the superiority, in terms of performance, of outsider-dominated boards (Dalton et al. 1998). Nevertheless, overall, there appears to be agreement that boards, at least in their control function in bodies such as the audit committee, should be dominated by outside directors.

Furthermore, recent discussions on board composition focus on *board diversity* (Milliken & Martins 1996). On the one hand, it increases the level and diversity of resources and perspectives available to a group. On the other, it is associated with higher levels of conflict, lower levels of integration, and interaction difficulties. Boards in particular may fall prey to these problems as they meet infrequently and do not work together closely. The most commonly researched variables of diversity include tenure (Vafeas 2003), age, educational and functional background (Golden & Zajac 2001), gender (Hyland & Marcellino 2002), and nationality (e.g., Ruigrok, Peck & Van del' Linde 2004). Overall, this research concludes that the influence of heterogeneity is not simple and direct, but rather complex.

Another stream of board composition research focuses on *interlocking directorates*, denoting situations where one director is simultaneously a member of the board or TMT of another company. Again, there are both advantages and disadvantages associated with this situation (Mizruchi 1996).

The benefits of interlocks are advocated mostly by the resource dependence perspective, which contends that firms may enjoy benefits of collusion, cooptation, lower transaction costs, access to information, and learning opportunities for corporate leaders (Keller 2003). Interlocks may also help to diffuse management practices. In terms of disadvantages, Keller (2003) posits that at the societal level, shortcomings include accumulation of social power, anti-competitive misuse, and inefficient resource allocation. At the firm level, they include limited board monitoring, conflicts of interest, and lack of directors' time.

The effect of interlocks is unclear however. While much of the literature focuses on the number of boards a director is sitting on concurrently, it has been suggested that the nature of the ties is more important. Carpenter & Westphal (2001), for example, have found that if a director sits on several boards, the degree to which their respective strategies are related has a significant impact on the director's involvement in a given firm's strategy.

Board Processes

Since the influence of boards with regard to the overall performance of an organisation is complex (Forbes & Milliken 1999), several authors deem it vital to understand the inner workings of a board (Roberts et al. 2005). It has also been suggested that matters surrounding the inner workings are significant (Lawrence 1997). This comes under the term »board processes« and includes »characteristics of boards« and »firm performance«. There is, however, no clear definition of this concept of »board processes«, though it may include easily observed aspects such as meeting frequency, working style, and information flow, or more complex issues such as cohesion, power, and agenda-setting (e.g., Finkelstein & Mooney 2003).

It is widely assumed that board structure and composition determine the board's ability to fulfil a certain role. Whether the board actually fulfils this role, however, is determined by board processes (Roberts et al. 2005). It is not enough that capable and knowledgeable directors sit on a board; they must actively use their knowledge and skills, and combine their experience and expertise in constructive ways (Forbes & Milliken 1999).

Board processes have still not been explored widely, mainly because the task of observing board processes is a very difficult one. Macus (2003) was the first author to integrate interaction into a theoretical model for boards, and to test his model using a case study. He also used a dynamic method, being the first to integrate changes over time in his model in terms of structures, compositions and demands on directors. This represents a significant advance from more static models which are unable to explain several famous corporate crises occurring in companies whose boards had been praised for their ideal composition a few years earlier. Macus (2003) cites the Enron scandal, which involved a board that complied with all of the best governance standards, but which was not able to catch up with new developments in the company, in particular with new complex financial vehicles.

Hermalin & Weisbach (2001) have also developed a dynamic model, which views the activities of a board as dependent on the power of the CEO and the length of time the CEO has been in office. This is based on the idea that long-term CEOs have demonstrated their abilities and have had more influence on the nomination and re-appointment of the current directors.

3. The Key Facts of M&A

By way of a broad introduction, mergers and acquisition are an effective way of aligning the structures of an economy experiencing fundamental changes both in global markets and with the arrival of new technologies. Even if recent increased global competition is not the primary reason for this process, it has accelerated its pace. Schumpeter's (1942) creative destruction of obsolete ideas and structures in order to create new combinations of productive capacities is incorporated in such adjustments. The cost of destruction would be bankruptcy. Now mergers and acquisition enable existing businesses and their employees to be retained with all their knowledge and experiences. In the »restructuring phase«, these resources are regrouped and optimised.

Contrary to public opinion, most mergers and acquisition do not restrict competition by creating large multinational companies, but rather enhance competition by promoting competitive pressures. Acquisitions are therefore not a route to large monopolies. As a matter of fact, new companies within new industries are continuously created. It must be mentioned, that the structures that are created by mergers are again exposed to competition. Even numerous tie-ups cannot withstand the force of competition. A fact that is often ignored is that acquisitions are accompanied by spin-offs (I further elaborate on this in the outlook chapter). These outsourced businesses lead again to new companies.

Judging by the headlines in newspapers, M&A are very often considered a threat due to the increased size of the newly created firms. In spite of this, acquisitions are not a threat. All sizes of firm can be managed successfully; however, different company sizes need different management structures and subsequently managers of a special calibre are required. Furthermore, acquisitions do not inherently lead to large monopolies, and size does clearly not mean strength (Malik 1999).

Despite an understanding of the above, acquisition success is not automatically generated. Corporate world realities have demonstrated that the timing of an M&A must be accurate and furthermore, managers must pay important attention to the acquisition integration process. All human aspects related to transformations followed by acquisition are of highest importance.

Acquisitions are typically carried out in a bid to enhance the competitiveness of a company. Ultimately, the consumers and customers are the main beneficiary. M&A therefore do not stifle competition; for example, acquisitions can lead to the restructuring of the core competencies of a company, or they can contribute to repositioning an organisation in the value chain when facing new global challenges. Nevertheless, mergers and acquisitions can only be an effective way of increasing a company's competitiveness if they are handled properly.

The past two decades prior to the financial crises have showed increasing activity in spectacular mergers and acquisitions. The prominent »M&A contests« between Rio Tinto and Alcan, Mannesmann and Vodafone, Daimler and Chrysler or Hewlett Packard and Compaq are striking examples.

In many ways, mergers and acquisitions are often unique business transactions. For most firms, acquisitions are relatively infrequent events. This implies that the companies have little experience and often rely heavily on outside help. Furthermore, M&A involve more outside assessment, and therefore increase the pressure to succeed. They typically require a large amount of resources, financially and, crucially, managerially. Contrary to other investment projects, there are no test runs and no milestones at which a firm may choose a different path, i.e. to modify or even abandon the acquisition project.

Considering their importance and scale, one would presume that acquisitions are well planned in order to create added value for the organisation. Despite this, acquisition, as one of a firm's most important investment decisions, more often destroys value rather than creating it by strengthening the long-term competitiveness of a company.

Furthermore, it is worth noting that acquisitions still prevail, as most companies still focus solely on shareholder value, which is based on profitability and on growth. Companies have focused on profitability over the last few years since the market crash in 2000–2002 and many companies got to the point where it became difficult to further increase their profitability (Guenter Mueller-Stewens, during interview). Currently, there is a shift in the corporate agenda towards the growth factor. Before the credit crunch, this was supported by the large amount of liquidity available on corporate balance sheets (Interview Mueller-Stewens).

Companies' excessive liquidity is not always viewed positively by shareholders and analysts, nor, ultimately, by the market. It is regarded as a lack of ideas from the management (Roman Boutellier, during interview). In order to avoid this and to act against a fall in share prices, several authors argue that this fact led to a momentum of increased acquisition activity in the corporate world, which was not necessarily accompanied by the desired success. In order to do effective deals and to increase the success rate, however, managers need more industry expertise (Guenter Mueller-Stewens, during interview).

One would expect managers to understand the important risk of failure and to therefore ensure that they have all the tools to effectively analyse and execute these transactions. Bad transactions not only waste management resources but destroy the values of both the target and acquiring firms.

Academics and well-known management thinkers have attempted to create formulas for successful M&A. Despite the tremendous amount of analysis regarding success factors, an explicative theory for the acquisition phenomenon does not yet exist. Still, the majority of acquisitions fail to create long-term value for companies and are subsequently often demerged (King et al. 2004). Ultimately, successful acquisitions require good and effective management and governance.

Major corporate failures based on abuses by CEOs over the last few years have led to intensified corporate governance discussions and regulations around the word. Subsequently, these developments appear to have caused board distrust of executive management and boards have become more sensitised and increasingly critical in approving management proposals.

Any board owes fundamental duty of care to its shareholders and this calls for board members to act prudently and on an informed basis with due deliberation before approving any decisions. Indeed, there are few, if any, strategies that are associated with as much immediate and ongoing risk to the company, target company, shareholders and stakeholders as major acquisitions.

In spite of this, many acquisitions fail to achieve the promised results, destroy trillions of USDs and lead to a psychologically destructive environment for employees. This begs the question: *what are the problems and do boards actually have the tools to act effectively in acquisitions?*

3.1 Developments in M&A Analysis

3.1.1 Mergers and Acquisitions (M&A)

A merger is defined for the purpose of this book as a combination of assets by two previously separate firms into a new single legal entity. In an acquisition or takeover, the control of assets is transferred from one company to another. In a complete takeover, the acquirer absorbs all the assets of the acquired company and the takeover target henceforth disappears.

As a matter of fact, the effective number of mergers in »mergers and acquisitions« is negligibly small. Complete acquisitions with a 100 % control account for more than half of all cross-border M&A.

Even when mergers are officially communicated between equal partners, in reality most result in one party dominating the other. As a matter of fact, the number of real, equal mergers is insignificant. Hence, for the purposes of the study, »M&A« and »mergers« are referred to by their ultimate meaning, as »acquisitions«.

There is a distinction in M&A between friendly and hostile takeovers. In friendly acquisitions, the board of the target firm agrees to the transaction. This may, however, be after a period of opposition to it. But the majority of acquisitions are friendly. Contrary to this, hostile acquisitions are undertaken against the will of the target company.

M&A are conventionally grouped into four categories, according to the direction of expansion and the relatedness of the businesses to be merged. Generally, the literature distinguishes between horizontal, vertical, concentric and conglomerate activities (Kootz 1996):

A *horizontal merger* occurs when two businesses are operating in similar or equal markets with similar or equal products. The merger objective is to expand the product portfolio or to increase the market share. A *vertical merger* occurs when companies which represent different stages of the value creation process merge. To increase the value added, either a business preceding or succeeding the stage in the value chain is integrated.

As companies follow the trend of reducing the activities along the value chain (Macharzina & Wolf, 2005), this type of merger is becoming less frequent. *A concentric merger* occurs when the merger is centred on a set of core competencies, such as product technology and marketing, with the aim to complement, to leverage the existing core competencies, or even to build up new competencies. A *conglomerate merger* is different in nature as it shows no relatedness in the value chain. Typically, these types of mergers are part of portfolio and diversification strategies.

Historical Analysis of Research on Acquisitions Management Phases

The acquisition process can be structured in four phases (Gilkey 1998). The initial phase is described as the targeting of the seller; the second phase begins when negotiations start; the third phase includes the implementation; and the final phase is described in literature as the integration of the target employees in the new configuration.

Hereafter, to simplify, the acquisition process is structured as two major management phases, **a pre-merger** and **a post-merger management phase.** Furthermore, the way in which research has developed on the topic of M&A is analysed and research deficits are identified.

3.1.2 Pre-Merger Management

Success of acquisitions has been analysed intensively. Both economical studies and financial theories have demonstrated that at least every other acquisition fails in terms of not fulfilling the expectations of wealth increase for shareholders (Mueller 1980, Jensen& Ruback 1983, Buehner 1990, Cartwright & Cooper 1992). Depending on consulting firms (BCG, KPMG, McKinsey) we find failure rates from 50–85 %.

The literature presumes that misguided motives of managers and their personal interest lead to the excessive failure rates of M&A. Indeed, there is evidence to suggest that managers act in their own interests, for example, to extend their power or increase status. By doing so, they overestimate their ability to successfully handle and lead an acquisition deal (Roll 1986, Jensen 1986, Mueller 1987, Merck, Schleifer & Vishny 1990).

Shareholders react negatively to M&A announcements because they deem their own interests to be in danger. Indeed, several authors demonstrated that this is the case particularly when acquisitions are not related to a firm's core businesses, since shareholders do not assume there will be a large synergy effect or complementary business relations (Berger & Ofek 1995).

The increased failure of M&A in practice during the 1970s meant that research started to focus more intensively on different aspects of planning (Humpert 1992, Coenenberg & Sautter 1988). This development was simultaneous with the beginning of scientific discussion of strategic planning in firms (Anstoff 1981). Hence M&A became issues of strategic planning. Acquisitions were understood as instruments for realising corporate strategies. During the 1970s and until the 1980s, European firms mostly followed a growth strategy based on diversification. The foundations for this were laid down by US example, for instance in the BCG Portfolio Matrix.

This development of diversification, however, was not hindered by regular, new research, which showed that more focused firms perform better than largely diversified, conglomerate firms (Rumelt 1982, Ravenscraft & Scherer 1987, Berger, Lang & Stulz 1994).

Cross-border M&A followed international acquisitions. Research, however, still focused on acquisition success. The research results based on the success of international as opposed to national acquisition, however, are vague (Doukas & Travlos 1988, Buehner 1991, Hitt, Hoskisson & Kim 1997). Some authors say that the possible reasons for unsuccessful international mergers are aspects like legal, market, and culture differences (Buehner 1991, Elsner 1986).

Other authors say that danger is inherent to removing management focus from organic growth and specifically innovation (Hitt, Hoskisson, Ireland & Harrison 1991). Contrary to this, Vermeulen and Barkema (2001) say that the short-term distraction of the management and the wasting of resources initiate firm restructuring and foster the competitiveness of the firm in the future. This conclusion may seem exaggerated, but the numbers of M&A continue to increase despite the huge amount of research in the 1980s and 90s on M&A failures.

Acquisition continuity has therefore been a challenge in strategic discussions and led to a shift of focus in M&A research. Instead of strategic planning, research now questioned the implementation of acquisitions and, as such, the focus moved to post-merger management. Alongside this shift, the theory approach also changed.

The resource-based view seemed to better explain the new focus compared to agency theory which became less important. The research shifted from an owner-oriented misbehaviour of management to that of core competences (Prahalad & Hamel 1990, Wernerfelt 1984, Peteraf 1993). With this, Porter's external strategy orientation shifted to one which was internal. Authors demonstrate that the adequate positioning of a firm in an industry, the ability to select appropriate resources (Makadok 2001) and to combine them (Teece 1987, Milgrom & Roberts 1995) is important for the success of the firm.

The new resource-based view also caused a re-evaluation of intangible assets (know-how, brand, reputation). Hence, research explained M&A failures as the lack of skills to mobilise intangible assets and to make use of them. In this way, organisational and management capabilities that are decisive in making an acquisition a success are at the centre of business research.

The resource-based view later induced discussion on disinvestments, recommending that firm parts that do not add value to a firm's core business should be sold off. Porter (1987) pointed out the impact on competitiveness of disinvestments in the context of acquisitions. Other authors deem disinvestments a result of acquisition failures (Ravenscraft & Scherer 1987, Allen et al. 1995). Lambrecht and Myers (2007) noted that takeovers serve as a mechanism to force disinvestment in declining industries. Their arguments lead to takeover transactions occurring mostly in industries that have experienced negative economic shocks.

Defenders of the resource-based theory criticise this »partial« view of M&A. They consider acquisition as only a part of the reconfiguration and restructuring process of a firm and they see acquisitions as a means of readjusting a firm's capabilities and resources (Nelson & Winter 1982, Ahuja & Katila 2001, Capron, Mitchell & Swaminathan 2001). Hence, disinvestments following acquisition reduce their negative character and are understood as part of a continuous process to increase competitiveness in the market.

3.1.3 Post-Merger Management

The question of how to successfully implement acquisition has been explored in various business and organisational theories (Gerpott 1993). It is a matter of finding the best way to eliminate organisational complications generated by acquisitions and to realise expected synergies.

Several authors suggest looking at compatible and complementary resources which need to be created with an acquisition. The process of creating these resources, however, can only be effectively managed if a strategic and organisational fit is present (Drucker 1981, Venkatraman & Camillus 1984, Datta 1991, Naman & Slevin 1993). Hence, the acquired target needs to be similar to the acquiring company in terms of its strategy and organisation. Such similarity should facilitate integration and decrease resistance from the employees.

The defenders of the »fit argument« say that there is a strong correlation between corporate culture similarities (common goals, values, employee attitudes) and the success of the integration process. In this context, the literature uses the concepts of assimilation and integration (Nahavandi & Malekzadeh 1998, Krystek 1992). While assimilation leads to cultural dominance of the acquiring firm over the target, integration should create a new identity by combining the best parts of each culture.

Regarding international, cross-border M&A, several authors discuss national cultural differences as factors for failure (Hofstede 1980, Barkema, Bell & Pennings 1996). There is a clear relationship between »national cultures' divergence« and »acquisition failure« (Chatterjee, Lubatkin, Schweiger & Weber 1992, Gersten, Soderberg & Torp 1998). Regarding R&D performance, Ahuja & Katila (2001) demonstrate that national cultural distance does not have a significant impact. This result conforms to the research of Weber, Shenkar & Raweh (1996), who did not find any specific integration difficulties in international acquisitions (see also Very, Lubatkin, Calor & Veiga 1997).

Following the considerations of cultural aspects in M&A, research becomes more differentiated and hence isolated issues within the integration process are analysed. In relation to this, several authors found that at the commencement of an acquisition, management strategists dominate the pre-merger phase (Jemison & Sitkin 1986, Haspeslagh & Jemison 1991). Nondisclosure, leadership image and different remuneration systems do endanger the integration success (Jemison & Sitkin 1986, Haspeslagh & Jemison 1991).

New research looks at acquisitions through a learning and evolutionary approach. Acquisitions are seen as a knowledge-based process and the resource allocation in this process is mainly built on human capital and on corporate governance considerations. Hence, the generation and transfer of implicit know-how is at the centre of research interest (the simple allocation of physical capital becomes secondary) (Kogut & Zander 1996).

Acquisition experience matters. Large, acquisition-oriented companies with a wide range of acquisition experience have an internal process based on guidelines which they use systematically for implementation. Implementation know-how might be a necessary criterion for a successful merger, but it is surely not the only one since the acquisition must first of all be based on an effective strategic decision.

As this brief historical overview shows, over time different schools have looked at various aspects of the issues. Notably, no multi-disciplined approach has been conducted to date. Peter Drucker's acquisition success factors, which are the topic of discussion in the next chapter, are relevant as his six pragmatic principles include the most critical elements. Before discussing and critically reviewing Drucker's six principles, the topic of acquisition success is presented.

3.2 Approaches to Acquisition Success

The subject of success is important when M&A are planned and when companies are integrated. When acquisitions are planned by managers, they tend to base their decisions on the benefit assessments of the acquisition. When companies have been integrated as a result of an acquisition, the management assesses if the deal has been a success or a failure. The management's behaviour is impacted by its evaluation of success.

Thus, future decisions are also affected by the perception of a given acquisition success. For instance, when management believes that an acquisition has been successful, it is more likely to make similar acquisitions and strategic moves in the future.

3.2.1 Previous Research on Acquisition Success

While literature has often dealt with the topic of acquisition success, previous publications have very often tackled research questions such as the success of particular M&A or which issues seem to impact, positively or negatively, their likely success. These research studies have been conducted in a variety of ways, the indicators of success have varied, and they have sometimes been implicit. A large number of different explanations have also been developed for the failure and success of M&A.

3.2.2 Different Success Indicators

In many event studies, stock prices served as indicators of success. Event studies became popular primarily in the 1980s. Several studies have measured success in acquisitions by using these methods since then. In the context of event studies, a company's stock price development is normalised. This helps to account for the price movements of all traded shares that bear risks that are similar. After the normalisation of the share price developments, unexpected returns are an indication of the reaction of the stock market with regard to the acquisition. In this approach, a positive or negative stock market reaction measures the success of an acquisition. Singh & Montgomery (1987), for example, have published such studies.

In many research studies, financial performance has been the indicator of success. Numerous studies have examined the financial performance of samples of M&A by using either regression analysis or other statistical methods. Several publications of this type were made before the event studies became popular at the beginning of the 1980s. Later in time for example, Schmidt & Fowler (1990) have published such studies. In some case studies, financial performance has also been an indicator of success (Vaara 1993).

A number of M&A studies based their success measurements on the evaluations of managers of the companies involved. Subsequently, based on the evaluations of these managers, numerical success indicators were constructed. Studies by Cannella & Hambrick (1993) and Datta (1991) are examples of such research.

Synergy has also often been used as an indicator of M&A success, in particular, in case studies. Vaara (1993) has published on this issue.

Further success indicators have also been used. Porter (1987) used a simpler success measurement in his publications: acquisitions were regarded as failures if they were later liquidated or divested.

It must be mentioned, however, that in many case studies the success indicators are not always explicitly defined. They were mentioned and described in an implicit way in the descriptions of the cases in question. The studies of Ghoshal & Haspeslagh (1990) and Haspeslagh & Jemison (1991) represent such examples in research.

In addition, several studies have used multiple indicators for success. Ravenscraft & Scherer (1987), for example, combined analyses of stock price and financial performance in their research.

3.2.3 Several Explanations for Failure and Success

The business relatedness or strategic fit elements within the acquisition context are the explanations that have probably received the most attention in research (Singh & Montgomery 1987). The main argument in this discussion has been that the potential value added from an acquisition is a function of the relatedness of the businesses of the merging companies. According to this view, M&A between organisations in similar businesses should provide more gains compared to acquisitions between companies in more unrelated businesses. However, the empirical research findings with regard to strategic fit have not been consistent (Mueller-Stewens, during interview).

Furthermore, the cultural fit argument of merging companies has also received broad attention (Chatterjee, Lubatkin, Schweiger & Weber 1992). The main point here is that cultural differences are likely to make the merger more difficult. Empirical research has found evidence that clearly supports the negative consequence of cultural differences with regard to the success of an acquisition.

In addition, several researchers have studied how the management affects success in the M&A process (Haspeslagh & Jemison 1991). A key argument here is that the success of an acquisition is very much dependant on the way the acquisition process is managed. From this point of view, skilful management can contribute to success in acquisitions. Likewise, the causes of failure in mergers and acquisitions are often managerial mistakes. The empirical findings are numerous and rich regarding management's impact on the success of mergers and acquisitions.

Several studies have also examined issues related to employee resistance and its subsequent effect on M&A success (Fowler & Schmidt 1989). The main argument is that contested acquisitions are likely to imply unproductive behaviour, a decline in morale and even acts of sabotage, and other behaviours that are not constructive or healthy for organisational performance. The research results strongly support this view.

It should also be mentioned that many other explanations have been provided for M&A success and failure. Some researchers have studied the impact of management turnover on acquisition success (Cannella & Hambrick 1993), while others have examined methods of financing as a factor influencing M&A success (Datta, Pinches & Narayanan 1992). Several analyses have also been conducted looking at the effect of the relative sizes of merging firms on acquisition success (Kusewitt 1985). Furthermore, studies have looked at the impact of prior experience in M&A on the outcome (Kusewitt 1985). The pre-merger performance of the acquiree and its effect on the deal success is also of research interest (Kusewitt 1985).

3.2.4 Conclusion

It is apparent that despite a tremendous amount of research we still face high rates of failure. While most analyses of M&A are conducted within the bounds of the researcher's field, Peter Drucker's principles for successful acquisitions are, in contrast, multi-dimensional, drawing from various different fields. Notably, almost all previous research focuses on management, and, in particular, the chief executive. To date, there is still a lack of the research with regard to the role of boards of directors in the acquisition process.

3.3 Normative Approach to M&A: Peter Drucker's Acquisition Success Factors

Making an acquisition successful necessitates close attention to human and organisational development. Integration activities require a fine combination of self-monitoring and action. A management which understands the benefits of successful integration will form important alliances with the relevant stakeholders of the target company throughout the integration process.

How do successful acquisitions differ from those that fail? The reasons for the failure, according to previous strategic management research on acquisitions, can be subdivided into the following groupings: *firstly*, the acquiring company targets the wrong firm; *secondly*, the acquired company is badly integrated; and *thirdly*, typically, too much is paid for the target company (Hayward 2002).

As we have already seen, the majority of acquisition studies deal with individual elements of the acquisition process such as the acquisition motivation, post-merger integration and other isolated areas. However, it is evident that a more comprehensive approach is required, which treats the critical M&A issues within a multi-dimensional framework. Drucker proposes that acquisition success is driven by numerous factors and their simultaneous impact on an acquisition. As this is the most comprehensive view of acquisitions to date, I have chosen to use his principles to analyse the case studies in order *to determine the leadership environments underlying their acquisition process.*

3.3.1 Peter Drucker's Six Acquisition Principles

»Very few acquisitions are successful. The reason why most acquisitions fail is because they disregard Peter Drucker's principles for successful acquisition.« (Fredmund Malik, during Interview)

Drucker's six principles for a successful acquisition:

1. For an acquisition to be successful it has to be founded on business strategy rather than financial strategy.
2. A fruitful acquisition has to be based on what the acquirer brings to the acquisition.
3. At the core of a successful acquisition there must be a common unity, for example marketing, the market, and technology or core competencies.
4. The acquirer must have respect for the target business, product, the customers of the acquired company, as well as its values.
5. The acquirer has to be ready to provide senior management to the acquired business within a reasonably short period, maybe 12 months maximum.
6. In a successful acquisition clear opportunities for advancement must be visible in both the acquired and the acquiring business.

3.3.2 Discussion of the Drucker Principles

»There are six simple rules for successful acquisitions and they have been followed by all successful acquirers since the days of J.P. Morgan a century ago.«
Peter Drucker, *The Wall Street Journal*, 15. 10. 1981.

Building on Paine & Power (1984), Drucker's success principles are based on the premise that the management's actions have a decisive impact on the success of acquisition.

Conversely, Porter (1980) argues that external factors such as the financial health of the target firm, the state of the industry and, more broadly, the economy significantly influence an acquisition's likelihood of success. Porter believes that acquisitions happen independently of the management's actions.

The interviews conducted for this book with renowned business leaders who created some of the most successful companies today, strongly support Paine & Power's assumptions.

1. For an acquisition to be successful it has to be founded on business strategy rather than financial strategy.

In essence, this means that successful acquisitions must be based upon a *well-developed business plan*, and *not solely on financial analyses*. The target company should match with the business strategy of the acquiring company. Without a match, there is every chance that failure will result.

Drucker offers the following by way of example (Drucker 2004): during the last decades of the 20th century the worst acquisition track record of any senior executive was that of Peter Grace, CEO of W.R. Grace. Drucker considered him a smart manager. He set out in the 1950s to develop a multinational enterprise but only through acquisitions that were financially based.

Grace put together the most able team of financial analysts and dispatched them around the world in search of potential acquisitions with low price-earnings ratios. Grace then purchased these firms thinking that these buys were at bargain prices. As a matter of fact, the financial analysis that Grace's team did before each buy was impeccable. The problem was, according to Drucker (2004), that the acquisitions were not based on any business strategy.

As a contrasting case, Drucker uses Jack Welch and GE as a prime example of a successful acquirer. Welch shaped the company in an impressive way during his tenure from the beginning of the 1980s until 2001, and to a large extent its expansion was based on acquisition. Almost all of GE's acquisitions were based on a sound and solid business strategy. This resulted in an impressive growth in the company's earnings as well as its market value (Drucker 2004).

2. A fruitful acquisition has to be based on what the acquirer brings to the acquisition.

An acquisition can only be successful if the acquirer carefully considers the way in which they could contribute to the target company. Crucially, the question is not whether the target firm will contribute to the acquirer. Drucker re-iterates the importance of this, noting further that the potential synergies are irrelevant from the buyer's point of view.

The way in which the acquiring firm can contribute to the target varies in that it could bring benefits in terms of technology, management, or even strength in distribution. Drucker specifies that this contribution must be more than just monetary; »Money by itself is never enough« (Drucker 2004). Hence, before making an acquisition, management must focus on contribution, not synergy.

As an example, Drucker mentions the acquisition of Citibank by Travelers. The acquisition was successful because Travelers conducted an in-depth analysis of the target company and planned, well in advance, what Travelers could offer Citibank in order to bring about a significant change in its operations.

Citibank had implemented its businesses successfully in almost all countries. At the same time, Citibank had built a management that was transnational. In terms of services and products, however, the bank was still quite a traditional bank. Its management and distributive capacity, however, exceeded the service and products that typical commercial banking delivered. Furthermore, Travelers had a strong position in terms of product and services, and considered itself capable of handling an increased volume of business based on Citibank's first class international distribution system and management (Drucker 2004).

One could argue, however, that Drucker's second principle seems limited because it neglects the potential contributions made by the target to the acquirer. Indeed there are cases where the management acquires a firm as much for what it can contribute to the target, as for what the target can contribute to the firm. This happens, for instance, when a target is purchased to increase the pool of resources, such as talented managers.

3. At the core of a successful acquisition there must be a common unity, for example, marketing, the market, and technology or core competencies.

Both companies, the acquirer and target, must share something in an area in which both firms are highly competent. Drucker argues that there must be a shared culture or, at the very least, some kind of cultural affinity. Like all successful diversification that is achieved through acquisition there is a presumption of »a common core of unity«.

Both companies must share either the same technology or markets. Sometimes, however, similarities in the production process are enough to fulfil the criterion. The same areas of expertise and experience, the same language and so on are elements that bring organisations together. Drucker (2004) argues that without a common core of unity, an acquisition cannot work, as the financial tie-up alone is not sufficient.

By way of example, Drucker cites the case of a large French company that has grown by taking over companies operating in all areas of luxury goods, be it fashion designers, champagne, exclusive watches or handmade shoes. At first sight, they appear to be unrelated businesses in a conglomerate, because the products do not seem to have much in common.

But Drucker argues that all of them are purchased by customers for the same reason: not the price or the utility of the products, but the status gained by owning them. Hence, all the acquisitions in this case have customer values in common, albeit each product is sold in quite different ways (Drucker 2004).

Bettis' (1981) study supports Drucker's rule. He analyzed large industrial companies and realised that the economic success is higher for companies in which hugely diverse areas of activity are related to a specific core competence. Based on his outcomes, Bettis argued that related diversified companies perform better than unrelated diversified companies with regard to their Return on Assets (ROA). Examples include companies like Johnson & Johnson or Bristol-Meyers.

Although this principle seems straightforward, Drucker's concept of »common core of unity« can be both broadly and narrowly defined. Large companies typically make several acquisitions. If an acquisition is not related, and therefore« does not share »a common core of unity«, a subsequent acquisition may share this concept with it and they then become related acquisitions.

Thus, despite the fact that Drucker's principle appears powerful and explicative, the rule is also ambiguous. Above all, defining and recognising a »common core of unity« can be more challenging to define in the moment, compared to retrospectively.

Malik's (1999, p. 252) view also supports the Drucker principle:

»The logic of a merger must relate to the market and-or to the technology and be anchored there. Everything else is accompanied by substantial additional risks. If the logic of a merger is not right, nothing will help. There is no way of leadership – not even to the highest level of sophistication – that could compensate a logical mistake within the basic architecture of a merger.« (Fredmund Malik)

4. The acquirer must have respect for the target business, product, the
customers of the acquired company, as well as its values.
There must be a »temperamental fit«.

A merger or an acquisition will be a failure unless the staff of the acquiring organisation respect the target company, its products, its market, and
ultimately its customers.

Drucker (2004) cites the example of several pharma companies which
acquired cosmetic firms, none of which turned out to be a success. He argues that »pharma people« and »cosmetic people« have different values. Bio-
chemists and pharmacologists are interested in disease and health in general. Conversely, »cosmetic people« deal with lipsticks and similar products.
Thus, pharmacologists do not have similar values to lipstick users.

If firms are not respectful or do not have a »comfortable« feeling about
the target, their businesses, product range, and ultimately their customers,
they will keep making the wrong decisions (Drucker 2004).

5. The acquirer has to be ready to provide senior management
to the acquired business within a reasonably short period,
maybe 12 months maximum.

Drucker posits that the acquiring company must be prepared to lose the
target firm's key people as these key people are accustomed to being leaders
and may not accept demotion to division managers. In the case where these
players have ownership or part ownership in the target, the acquisition will
make them rich. As a consequence, they will not continue their duties for
the firm if they do not enjoy them or like the change. The acquirer must also
be sensitive to the fact that the professional managers of the target company,
who do not have an ownership stake, will usually be headhunted by other
companies, making the shift easy for them.

In the case of a management departure where the acquiring company
is not prepared to provide new management itself, the recruitment of new
people is difficult and rarely succeeds (Drucker 2004).

This is particularly relevant in the case of a chief executive who founded
the target business. In some cases this chief executive has actually initiated the acquisition process. This CEO may expect the acquiring firm to
implement the personnel changes that he is reluctant to do. Such changes could include, for example, firing a well-settled colleague and friend,
who is underperforming professionally because the corporate environment

has changed, leaving this person outgrown by his previous job description (Drucker 2004).

The attempt to keep senior management is usually of higher importance than succession planning for those who leave. It is therefore usual for an acquired company to try to retain the management post-takeover. Malik notes particularly the social implications for a target management. An acquisition can create job insecurity for a target management which may be harmful. Indeed, matters related to human relations in acquisition are important. The top managers of a target company see their status in their private social lives damaged due to the loss of power and responsibility in their jobs.

It is interesting to see that authors like Hayes (1979) have already shown in early studies that in almost all cases where the key people of the target management were retained the pre-acquisition negotiations actually happened on both social and business levels. It is very interesting to note that the author found out that discussion typically included the wives of the managers.

In order to retain the target's top management, it would therefore seem instrumental for the acquiring company to stress considerable involvement of the target's management in negotiations.

6. In a successful acquisition clear opportunities for advancement must be visible in both the acquired and the acquiring business.

With regard to his final principle, Drucker states that during the first twelve months of the acquisition, it is vital that a significant number of key people from both the acquiring and target company receive significant job promotions. These promotions need to happen across the companies, meaning the promotion of target company managers to new positions at the acquiring company and vice versa.

The reasoning behind this promotion activity is powerful, as it shows and convinces the business staff in each firm that the changes to come will bring them new opportunities. Drucker states that it is very important to be aware that although the acquired business is now legally part of the acquiring firm, politically, the managers of the target become an »us« determined to defend their business against »them«, the staff and management from the acquiring company.

Similarly, managers in the acquiring company behave and think in the same terms. These invisible and impenetrable barriers can last a whole generation, thus it is vital to promote key people on both sides within the very first months of an acquisition. This enables managers from »both sides« to see the acquisition as a personal opportunity. In fact, this principle applies not only to top managers or those near the top, but also to the younger executives and professionals (Drucker 2004).

Conclusion of Drucker's Six Principles

The stock market is highly aware of the difficulty of acquisition integration. Thus, in numerous instances, reports of large deals in the news lead to significant drops in the acquiring company's share price. Despite this fact, to date, managers of both acquiring and target companies continue to ignore these basic principles, as do the bankers in agreeing to finance the acquisition, because to a large extent they still base the deal on financial rather than business concerns.

In conclusion, managers appear to be able to impact acquisition outcomes by acquiring information and planning thereon. Thus, ultimately, managers' skill and experience enable successful acquisitions. The quick implementation of a merger or acquisition as well as the high priority of human relations issues are instrumental to the merger's success. Hence, although risks are inherent to all acquisitions, following Drucker's principles significantly reduces them and creates competitive companies in the long-term.

Thus, using these effective acquisition success principles as tools of investigation, the next chapter outlines and begins the analysis of the »leadership environments« fostered at Nestle and Swissair, and the way in which these have precipitated a history of successful or unsuccessful acquisitions.

4. Prime Examples of Good and Bad Acquisition Management

4.1 Board Management Background of the Case Studies

No single approach to board management works in every social or economic circumstance. In spite of this, in the last few decades, American corporate governance approaches have become dominant as a style of board management because of the globalisation of capital markets which are largely dominated by America. These styles are often unsuitable to the various contexts of international firms.

With regard to the following two case studies analysed in this chapter, they are both multinational companies based in Switzerland and under Swiss law. The board system in Switzerland differs, for example, from the system of a unitary board in the American-British business world or the strict dual board system of Germany.

Switzerland's Code of Obligations leaves companies quite a bit of discretion in designing and optimizing their top structures (Biland 1989, p. 18). The law requires firms to have a minimum of one board, consisting of at least a president and a secretary (Art. 712OR). In principle, the board is in charge and accountable for all tasks that, according to law or the articles of association, involve the corporation's day-to-day business dealings and do not fall under the responsibility of the general assembly (Art.716,1OR). The directors can, however, delegate duties to the »delegate of the board« or to other »directors«. In the case of delegation, the board is responsible for the »business of the firm, to the extent that is it does not delegate it to management« (Art. 716 2OR).

»(...) the governing board, according to Swiss Law, has ultimate responsibility (»Oberleitung«). This means that the board normally runs the business.

In practice, of course, that isn't very realistic; in a large company a board of 15 people can't run the business. As a rule, the board delegates the management function to the so-called »delegate of the board«. If this is the case, then this delegate has a relatively strong legal authority and the Swiss type of governing board has a reduced responsibility, similar to a German supervisory board. In this case, the governing board has re-assigned its responsibility. Though it never goes so far as in Germany where a management board can buy a company for 10 billion without consulting the governing board.

This isn't the case in Switzerland. Here the board not only decides on the nominations for the director generals but is also involved in anything that concerns the management as well as important strategies and acquisitions.« (Helmut Maucher, during interview)

As such, Swiss firms can choose from a continuum of systems, depending on the extent and modus of delegation. Generally, three models stand out (Bleicher 1989, Forstmoser 1996).

The *first model* is based on the premise that the management of the firm is being handled by inside board members and the supervision is handled mostly by outside board members, the American and British one-tier/unitary board system can thus be realised.

The *second model* depends on the board delegating the majority of the firm's management to a non-board member CEO. In this way, the German dual board system with strict separation of management and supervision is emulated.

The *last model* is based on the delegate of the board assuming much of the power and authority, through holding the chairperson position simultaneously. This model conforms closely to the French system of a President Directeur General.

These three models, however, can only be implemented to the extent that the board retains the non-transferable tasks of ultimate direction and the right to withdraw its delegation at any time.

In practice, most listed companies in the Swiss case adopt a two-tier board structure, which is more similar to the German model than the American-British model of a unitary board.

The *first tier*, the board of directors, is comprised mostly of non-executive directors and is responsible for supervising management and shaping the company's long-term strategy (Biland & Zahn 1998). The *second tier*, the management board (sometimes referred to as the executive committee), consists only of managers and is in command of daily operations.

Swiss firms are often arranged so that the CEO is the delegate and vice chairperson of the board, complemented by an external board chairperson (Forstmoser 1996).

4.2 Important Background Information about the Case Studies

Analysing the following two case studies seems particularly appropriate, as both were conducted under *almost identical situational conditions*, a unique occurrence which has probably never happened previously in economic history.

Both case studies are about typical large corporations. While Nestlé was larger than the Swissair Group in absolute numbers, both were predominantly multinationally active companies in which the board had to be capable of dealing with the challenges of the multi-cultural elements of their business activities.

Importantly, both entities were subject to the same legal jurisdiction, and therefore had the same juridical and political framework for their corporate governance. The acquisitions covered in the case studies occurred during the same timeframe and both boards were highly respected and composed of personalities who were seen as capable of fulfilling their duties. Both companies followed, in principle, the same strategy, which was forced growth through acquisition, but where the Swissair Group failed dramatically, Nestlé became one of the most successful companies in the world.

With regard to the Nestlé case I have conducted, besides internal document sources which have never been seen by the public, a vast number of interviews with board members. This was not the case with Swissair, as the trial was taking place at the time of the study and many board members were not willing to discuss sensitive information. Moreover, board members generally do not want to talk openly about failures although, of course, they are pleased to talk about successes.

Therefore, in the case of Swissair, along with a certain amount of interview material, the primary analysis was of the Ernst & Young (E&Y) report and other available company documents. Indeed, the E&Y document functions as a vital source of facts in determining if particular organisational parties, like the board of directors, precipitated the decline of the firm. Not all of the important materials were at their disposal and E&Y were open about the fact, but despite this, they posit that the accessible documents were enough to work with in terms of their report. Several thousand pages made up this document, which examined a huge quantity of material accessible to the audit and consulting firm (invoices, reports, documents to do with the organisation, etiquette for meetings etc.).

A few business leaders, in particular from Swissair, wished to remain anonymous due to the fact that they were facing legal claims at the time of the interviews. In order to protect their identities their names were not disclosed. On the whole, however, most agreed to their opinions being published.

4.3 Remarks about the Period of Focus in the Two Case Studies: the Era of Chairmen During the Period of Acquisitions

When a board supervises a firm, their duties as decision makers are of the highest importance. Board members act for shareholders as their voted representatives. The more wide-ranging duties frequently assigned to the president or chairperson in firm regulations include the deciding vote in a draw scenario, signing the annual report, and meeting etiquette and conduction. Furthermore, it is considered the norm for the president to have a more proactive approach to duties and participation. Although the rest of the members fulfilled their board duties alongside other tasks, in Swissair and Nestlé both made the president's position a full-time job. Moreover, between 1990 and 1997, the chairman in Nestlé was simultaneously also the CEO.

Fundamentally, the chairman ought to guide his board members in terms of business, leadership, social skills and personality (Hilb 2002, p. 65). This enlarges the chairman's responsibilities in terms of the health of the firm for the stakeholders' advantage. Thus, the following two best and worst case scenarios look at their presidents' periods of office and attempt to derive deductions about their tenure. Both time frames are characterised by the organisations' implementation of numerous acquisitions.

4.4 Best Case Scenario: Nestlé

This case study investigates the thriving company of Nestlé under Helmut Maucher which was also a time in which a great number of acquisitions were made. Nestlé's history is briefly examined and then the way in which the company handled acquisitions is analysed.

As a brief note on sources, this chapter has been enriched hugely by interview material. Unexpectedly, many board members agreed to long and in-depth interviews. The opinions and insights of these renowned business leaders have valuable significance. Important entrepreneurial business figures who were not directly involved with Nestlé, such as Thomas Schmidheiny, were also interviewed, including several anonymous leading board members of other multinational companies. Interestingly, the consistency of their attitudes in the interviews with the CEO's and the board's is highlighted and supported by documents and minutes from the time. Indeed, these important papers constitute one of the unique aspects of the analysis and a few have been selectively integrated into this chapter.

4.4.1 Description of the Firm

At nearly 150 years old, Nestlé is the largest food corporation on earth in terms of sales. The company is a leading player in the coffee and pet food industries and one of the biggest bottled-water manufacturers. Conducting business in nearly every nation on the globe, Nestlé has almost 280,000 employees. In 2009, Nestlé enjoyed sales of USD 107.6 billion, and a net income of USD 10.4 billion.

4.4.2 Corporate Governance Structure and Its Effectiveness

Board-Management Relationship

In order to ensure Nestlé remained competitive worldwide, at the beginning of the 1990s Helmut Maucher started to make alterations to the way the company was run and also within the organisation. He launched a pair of »strategic business groups« to guide a number of product group strategies, which were divided into seven units (Helmut Maucher, during interview). This was in order to advance on his previous efforts to stop centralization.

Senior executives with similar power to the zone operations' managers, but not the same responsibility, led these groups. Maucher also created the position of COO for Food to assume responsibility for keeping product orientation on track and for coordination of operations in terms of general managers. At headquarters, Maucher radically reduced the size of the previously influential central technical department and various functional groups (Philippe de Weck, during interview).

At TMT level, this restructuring resulted in the formation of a core constituting one head and ten senior managers working from Vevey. Under Maucher's watchful control, they became the most important general management committee in the firm (Helmut Maucher, during interview).

Maucher also remoulded the culture of leadership at Nestlé and expressed his innovative approach as *»commitment of management and involvement of staff«* (Bruno de Kalbermatten, during interview). If the TMT worked less through capability and power and more by intentionally generating added value for the firm through leadership, it would also involve and inspire their employees.

Maucher tried to figure out at what point he added value or provided gainful input in the debate; otherwise, he handed over matters even when, technically, the final choice ought to have been made by him (Bruno de Kalbermatten, during interview).

It is enlightening to look at Maucher's approach to corporate governance as the key issue, one which *»needs more principles and fewer detailed regulations«* as these regulation do not fit every company (Helmut Maucher, during interview).

In terms of structure, the function of the CEO and chairman and the eventual fusion of these two roles he considers an »overrated« problem, more dependent on who is available, and on whether plans and balanced correlations are in place. The stipulations are that there should be a committee with *»independent, strong people who can act if the man in question abuses their trust or does not work out«* and a back-up plan in the case of something happening to the leader (Maucher, during interview).

Furthermore, in contrast to many other firms, Maucher informed the board annually of his long-term succession plans, whom he thought suitable to replace him as CEO (in the long-run or in the case of an incident) and his recommendations in terms of what needs to be done. If these conditions exist, then *»the pulling together of roles is useful and administratively less complicated«* (Helmut Maucher, during interview).

Importantly, this does not mean that a complete concentration of power develops; whether as chairman or delegate, one has to *»share power always with the board«* and with a duty to report, alongside clear rules as to who decides what, the balance is never lost and *»this so-called omnipotence doesn't exist«* (Helmut Maucher, during interview).

Board Committee

Nestlé's board was structured so that a smaller committee within the board met every month to discuss business matters. In his interview, Maucher stated that he believed in having as few committees as possible and was against the »trend« to have two committees on each board, preferring the following structure: a general committee to make preliminary decisions; an audit committee, to give the board the opportunity to check everything; and a remuneration committee, which was partially the same as the general committee only smaller (Helmut Maucher, during interview).

As illustrated in the coming chapters, the committee was quite involved in all business aspects and worked in close cooperation with the CEO, providing support and asking for information. With regard to the board committee, de Weck further stated in his interview that:

»I believe that the board committee was a good way to work. The board of directors' role was less important as they had only six sessions per year and because it had many members at the time. Discussions weren't as easy.« (Philippe de Weck, during interview)

Board Culture

Maucher described a culture in which lively debate and the expression of concerns, in particular over issues of long-term risk, were promoted (Helmut Maucher, during interview). He was clearly a hugely respected personality who always brought the whole board on side:

»The people trusted me more every year because I didn't deceive them. I never lied to them. I was logical in what I told them. The people knew that I'm not an adventurer because I never took excessive risks. For this reason, they have always agreed with what I've done.« (Helmut Maucher, during interview)

This culture of a proactive interest in the views of all involved even extended to acquisition. When a new firm was acquired, Maucher immediately travelled there to talk with everybody about how they felt good changes could be made and to convince them of the integrity of his leadership. An example of this was the emphasis he placed on making opportunities visible for all personnel in the Group.

Moreover, Maucher always prioritised the opinions and expertises of those on his board above external consultants and analysts, believing that those closest to the company had the most specific knowledge. This was a huge vote of confidence for all involved and showed the members that their contributions were respected and highly valued.

4.4.3 M&A Strategy: A Complete Success

Helmut Maucher's Reign: a Time of Multiple, Large-scale Acquisitions

When Maucher became »administrateur délégué« in 1981 Nestlé's finances were crumbling. Despite the firm's speedy growth in emerging markets, growth in industrialized countries slowed, the cost of oil increased, the cost of cocoa and coffee beans rose dramatically, and the Swiss currency appreciated. Maucher's new policies had an important impact on Nestlé's *modus operandi* and his tenure is the focus of this work. He spearheaded two ways to improve the firm's financial position:

He cut the numbers of employees in the headquarters, giving more power to operating units, which decreased overheads. Furthermore, he lead a succession of large acquisitions and by 1984, he was leading one of its most significant, instigating the foundation of the current concentration on organic growth.

In this way, the company had secured a presence in a number of areas in different geographical regions, and now Nestlé had fewer products or nations it still wanted to expand to. It was also getting more expensive to acquire firms and fears of antitrust were increasing. In the late 1990s, therefore, the company's acquisition speed relented and the firm moved into organic growth.

In his interview, Maucher pointed out that all of their acquisitions were later successful. He thought that this was due to the fact that they had *»never entered a venture by taking a leap of faith, we always knew what we were buying«* (Helmut Maucher, during interview). Moreover, he thought that they had avoided failures by making judgements on a realistic and factual basis and by buying firms within their own sector, and only those that they understood well. As proof of the success of this policy he added, *»McKinsey claims two thirds of acquisitions go wrong – this wasn't the case for us«* (Helmut Maucher, during interview).

Maucher became involved with Nestlé at a crucial moment. Despite a lengthy profitable period, Nestlé experienced a decrease in profits around the 1980s. The Argentinean subsidiary of the firm had unparalleled losses in the early 1980s and it was a shock to the old-fashioned top management that this was a direct result of bad management. Moreover, they were being boycotted by certain bodies because of an outcry over infant formula. It was a mental shock to the firm to have hostile public exposure, when they were so used to their image as a smart company making healthy products.

When Maucher became chief executive, after almost three decades of working for the Group, he initiated a programme of instant modifications, which were necessary given the situation. The Nestlé culture had grown old-fashioned; it was overly bureaucratic, overly structured, and was suffering from an excess of systems and rules. While he disposed of most of it, Maucher tried to retain the firm's culture, values and individual style.

Highlighting its redundancy, Maucher threw out the monthly books which constituted the various subsidiaries' financial reports and replaced them with, essentially, one page. He contended that staff counts, inventories, cash, sales and the market head's individual thoughts were the few vital gauges for a smart manager to understand the state of the business (Helmut Maucher, during interview).

Fundamentally, the bureaucratic systems had created a predicament in which everyone was happily ignorant of what was going on, and were unwilling to change as a consequence. By reorganising and shifting operations away from the centre, Maucher was making quite radical changes. Simultaneously, he gave headquarters more responsibility in terms of research, matters of strategy, financial issues and other matters over which headquarters ought to be in control.

When Maucher became involved, the company's position in terms of working capital was bad. Before he got to work, there was an annual cash drain of half a billion CHF, excluding acquisitions. By educating individuals about it and altering some fairly straightforward matters, millions in cash were instantly available. Before long, he could have several billion readily available in cash and at the same time acquire new companies. In this way, Maucher succeeded by understanding what was vital, and by creating appropriate and exact aims and priorities (Philippe de Weck, during interview).

Maucher attempted to increase the firm's competitiveness in terms of products and geography, on the basis of vastly better cash flow generated by fresh management policies. Although it had already begun a few years before, the 1990s was a period of growth by means of strategically minded acquisition (Philippe de Weck, during interview).

The main aims of the acquisitions were to secure the Group as a global leader in particularly high growth areas such as confectionary, chocolate and mineral water, and to drastically increase the Group's share in the American market (Helmut Maucher, during, interview). They also sent out the vital message that the sleeping giant had awoken.

The company had thus secured a presence in a number of areas in different countries, and now had fewer products it lacked and fewer markets to enter. It was also getting more expensive to acquire firms and fears of anti-trust were increasing. In the late 1990s, therefore, the company's acquisition rate slowed and the firm moved into a period of organic growth.

The Relationship Between the CEO and Board

»I've never come across a company that ran well with a bad CEO because the board was working so well. On the other hand there are a number of companies that work where the board is mediocre but the CEO is very good.« (Helmut Maucher, during interview)

Maucher's board supported this by saying that, »*the best acquisitions we have made at Nestlé were all done by the CEO as the board can't do that*« (A2, during interview) and Philippe de Weck confirmed in interview that »*he did everything and we trusted him, but still everything was discussed*« (Philippe de Weck, during interview).

Maucher believes that the CEO is the key person in the company because he has the greatest understanding of the business. To his mind, the board cannot lead a company if it only comes to the business every four weeks, especially if they are specialists like bankers and lawyers with no experience in the company. The CEO, however, possesses all of the relevant information and experience. Maucher concludes that the board must be informed and approve the CEO's actions, but ultimately »*the quality of the CEO is the decisive factor, not only in terms of intelligence but character – the role needs both personality and professional intelligence*« (Helmut Maucher, during interview).

As Bruno de Kalbermatten noted during his interview, this thinking carries through to strategy: »*the CEO should be a ›driving force‹ and not an ›administrating force‹*«. Maucher also believes that the development of strategy clearly lies with the CEO who »*investigates the potential project with his managers and if he deems it worthwhile he will present it to the board, which then makes a decision*« (Helmut Maucher, during interview).

The board can ask questions and give opinions but »*if the board expresses another opinion, and I can't convince them, then the strategy needs to be changed accordingly«* (Helmut Maucher, during interview). Maucher regards the board firstly as a contributing body, secondly as a controlling body and finally as a body for important decisions (Helmut Maucher, during interview). It's important to acknowledge, however, that the final power rests with the board. As Maucher revealed, the CEO cannot do certain things without the board as without them a project cannot go forward.

During his tenure, Maucher's independent spirit was crucial. He was not interested in appeasing the board, or personal politics; for example, if the board rejected his proposals three times, he would resign as *»I would assume that they have a problem with me and not with the projects«* (Helmut Maucher, during interview).

The board seemed to fully support the idea of the CEO as the driving force. Bruno de Kalbermatten, one of Maucher's board members, quoted Maucher's book »Marketing ist Chefsache«[2] concurring with Maucher's view that marketing, in terms of satisfying organisational objectives, should be dealt with by the top leadership level. Moreover, he felt it was *»an essential element – there have been some exceptions at Nestlé but with Helmut Maucher, everything was fine«* (Bruno Bruno de Kalbermatten, during interview).

He admitted that there would be complications if the board began wondering if the CEO was really right for the job, for example, *»because he's sick, because he's on too many boards of directors, because some acquisitions failed etc«* (Bruno de Kalbermatten, during interview). Ultimately, in de Kalbermatten's mind, *»there's no absolute rule«* but at Nestlé a *»strong trust«* between the board and Maucher meant there were never any problems (Bruno de Kalbermatten, during interview).

Clearly it worked so well at Nestlé because Maucher was a strong CEO, committed to the long-term well being of Nestlé and its customers and nothing else. He never had a contract. Everyone's position was determined annually and Maucher was happy with this. A sense of mutual respect and trust prevailed.

Maucher assumed that *»even if we have an argument, I will be treated decently, for example, in terms of my pension and so on«* and found that there were never any problems with this at the company (Helmut Maucher, during interview). Another reason he liked this was that he felt *»the others have to be free to split from me if they don't agree with me anymore«* and lastly, it was vital that legal problems did not interfere because his *»position as chief executive was too important for the company«* (Helmut Maucher, during interview).

---

2 English title: »Leadership in Action«

This is quite a different perspective in light of the way other companies bind their CEO with many legal contracts. In fact, CEOs often ask for these legal assurances, including golden parachutes and so on. Maucher pointed out, however, that roles were very clearly delineated in Nestlé's constitution, stipulating the CEO's responsibilities and in which decisions the committee or the whole board needed to be involved. It also stated what rights the CEO had to information, that no CEO could be elected without the consent of the board and that »*the whole process of nomination and dismissal was a board matter*« (Helmut Maucher, during interview).

Nestlé under Maucher was an exemplary case of effective management. Looking at other firms' failure in acquisition, Maucher concluded that the chief executives often follow other interests, sometimes their own, which are not in line with the long-term interests of the company. He stated that while it was preferable to avoid interfering with the CEO's plans, »*if the CEO has a different agenda and cooks his own soup all the time, or doesn't really understand the business, then the board has to react immediately*« (Helmut Maucher, during interview).

In terms of the board recognising when a CEO is not behaving properly, Maucher pointed out that at Nestlé the board had the right composition of »*clever people*« to recognise such problems quickly:

»I had a Mr. Gerber, who rescued Zurich and Roche. I had a Mr. Kalbermatten, he runs his own company, and knew how it worked. I had a Mr. Gut, who was president of CS and I had a Mr. Leutwyler, who was president of Nationalbank. In other words, all of these people had life experience, common sense and were independent enough to have reacted immediately should things have gotten out of hand.« (Helmut Maucher, during interview)

Philippe de Weck supported this idea, that personality is more important than specific industrial knowledge for board members: »*in certain areas it's useful to have a technician, a finance person or a lawyer, but not everybody needs to be a specialist*« (Philippe de Weck, during interview).

Furthermore, the board also acted through the board committee as an additional watch dog of the CEO's activities; the committee was much closer to the business than the board as a whole because they met on almost a monthly basis and received every report. As Maucher pointed out, they had all of the information and the support of the audit committee. With continuous access to information on press, investor conferences and reports on profit, turnover and flow of staff, »*if they don't realise when things go wrong then we have the wrong committee*« (Helmut Maucher, during interview).

The advisory committee, as understood through interviews with the board members, was not only a watch dog but also a body that provided valuable advice and followed important business activities closely. In terms of whether Nestlé's board had a monitoring function or an active advising function, Bruno de Kalbermatten said in interview that it depended on the size of the firm. In Nestlé's case, he reported that the advisory committee (5–6 people) within the board (15–18 people) fulfilled both roles of monitoring and advising.

The committee (Maucher, de Weck, Gerber, de Kalbermatten, and Leutwyler) were often in touch with regional directors that came and reported about their activities, and they had decision making power for acquisitions of up to CHF 500 million, »*which is a significant amount*« (de Kalbermatten, during interview). In fact, Bruno de Kalbermatten only felt he »*started to play a part*« when he became a member of the committee, because the board of directors was »*only a recording organ, a guarantee of the company's seriousness*« and it was the committee that made decisions, not the board of directors although, of course, their approval was sought (Bruno de Kalbermatten, during interview).

The members met 8–10 times a year and were usually external apart from Maucher. De Kalbermatten said that they had good, trusting relationships as »*5 or 6 people can have a discussion around a table. At the board, there's 15 people and the general directors, so that's 25 people. You can't have discussions this way*« (Bruno de Kalbermatten, during interview).

In Bruno de Kalbermatten's interview, he thought that the best way to monitor the CEO was by focusing on results because the board is too far away from the daily business to know what is going on.

Academic research talks about »management hubris« where one success after another eventually leads to an overestimation of the management's capabilities resulting in a deal, in this case, an acquisition, which is too big. Bruno de Kalbermatten thought there was »*no rule*« for avoiding this situation but »*at Nestlé, as long as Maucher was there, we never had this kind of problem*« (Bruno de Kalbermatten, during interview). Thomas Schmidheiny, a renowned industrialist, thought more particularly, that:

»What distinguishes Mr. Maucher – and I have tried to live up to this – is that he remains modest despite all the success. People simply believe him. He has remained credible and modest. He hasn't become a megalomaniac.« (Thomas Schmidheiny, during interview)

In terms of how the board recognises if the CEO is informing them in a correct and transparent manner, Maucher states that his board had the right calibre of personalities, it is »*a question of judgement, a question of personal experience, it is about asking the right questions*« (Helmut Maucher, during interview).

An audit committee also had full access to all information. Furthermore, the board received comprehensive and substantial strategy papers every year in which Maucher presented his reflections as well as a »confidential note« in addition to the business plan, a paper describing the crucial activities of the previous year which was a kind of »*photograph that captures all developments in every country, products, revenues, costs etc*« (Helmut Maucher, during interview).

Everyone was very well informed with these two documents and they were discussed by the board, questions were asked and the »*CEO and his director general had to answer*« (Helmut Maucher, during interview). Maucher finished on this by pointing out the need to be able to »*differentiate between delegating a lot and not being able to run a business*« (Helmut Maucher, during interview).

The following internal board document is highly revealing in that it shows how diligently the board committee was working as well as how involved and informed they were on the matter. It also shows both the proactive nature of the board in seeking information and the responsiveness of the CEO in providing further information (see Figure 1).

Interestingly, in the interviews with other leading CEOs and chairmen as well as members of Nestlé's board at the time, opposing views were aired on this subject. A leading CEO of another Swiss multinational company said:

»I don't know if you know how the board meetings in Nestlé took place, but only when the board met did members receive their files and then they had to give them back after the meeting.« (A1, during interview)

Philippe de Weck, a board member who was on the committee during Maucher's reign concluded differently:

»We went to Vevey the day before, usually for one day, or at least half a day, during which we only studied the projects, and then there was a session the next day. This way, through the project's study, the session was adequately prepared for.« (Philippe de Weck, during interview)

De Weck did concede, however, that the documents for study were not sent beforehand to the board committee members but rather:

Matran, le 1er décembre 1982

Monsieur Helmut Maucher
Administrateur-Délégué
Nestlé S.A.
Avenue Nestlé

1800 Vevey

Cher Monsieur,

Je voudrais tout d'abord vous confirmer combien je trouve que les documents à l'intention du comité du conseil ont fait de progrès. Ils sont beaucoup plus synthétiques et portent sur les points essentiels. Je vous en remercie et vous en félicite.

A l'heure actuelle, il y a un seul point sur lequel mon information n'est pas tout à fait celle que je voudrais : c'est l'information sur la naissance, la vie et la mort des produits, si je puis m'exprimer ainsi.

Sans doute avons-nous une considérable documentation sur les produits en groupe : nous savons l'évolution du chiffre d'affaires, des tonnages, nous avons des indications que tel ou tel produit avance ou recule dans tel ou tel pays. Mais c'est très global, très statistique et très difficile à synthétiser.

Il serait intéressant de suivre :

- ce qui meurt
- ce qui est condamné
- ce qui naît
- ce qui marche normalement
- ce qui est un succès.

./.

Figure 1: Correspondence Philippe de Weck to Helmut Maucher

- 2 -

Nous n'avons non plus à notre échelon presque aucune indication sur l'activité de la concurrence, sinon par les coupures de journaux du document jaune. Mais là aussi la synthèse est impossible à faire par nous.

Peut-être est-il difficile de faire cette information par écrit. Pourrait-on alors la faire par des exposés ? Par exemple un groupe de produits par séance.

Il n'y a jamais d'exposés dans nos séances sur des sujets définis. C'est un peu dommage, les exposés permettent aussi de mieux connaître et mieux juger les membres de la direction générale. Qu'en pensez-vous ?

Je vous remercie de l'attention que vous voudrez bien apporter à ces modestes suggestions et vous prie de recevoir, cher Monsieur, mes très cordiaux messages.

Figure 1: Next page

Ja ng

HELMUT MAUCHER
ADMINISTRATEUR DÉLÉGUE
NESTLÉ S.A.

AVENUE NESTLÉ
1800 VEVEY (SUISSE)
TEL. 021/51 01 12

Le 14 décembre 1982
HM/JSR

Monsieur Philippe de Weck

Les Rappes

1753 - Matran

Cher Monsieur de Weck,

J'ai bien reçu votre lettre du 1er décembre me
faisant part de vos suggestions concernant l'information et la discussion au sein du Comité du
Conseil.

Je suis d'accord avec vous pour penser qu'une
information sur la gamme des produits, sur l'activité de la concurrence, pourrait être très
utile. Mes collègues et moi allons réfléchir
quant à la façon d'introduire ce type d'information dans nos séances à partir de l'année
prochaine.

Je profite de la présente pour vous souhaiter,
ainsi qu'à votre famille, un Joyeux Noël et pour
vous adresser mes voeux les meilleurs pour 1983.

Je vous prie de croire, Cher Monsieur de Weck,
à l'assurance de mes meilleurs sentiments.

H. Maucher

Figure 1: Next page

»We had to go and check them on the in situ. They were not going out. And those who didn't live in the area even had to stay overnight in Vevey.« (Philippe de Weck, during interview)

The rationale would appear to be based on gathering members in a specific place to ensure the material was studied properly, despite the fact that this was often inconvenient and, one could argue, a little controlling, but Maucher made the point that this was also done for reasons of secrecy.

Nevertheless, another prominent business leader from outside the company, who was aware of the *modus operandi* of the committee, was outraged by the extremely limited preparation time available:

»Everyone at Nestlé, according to Swiss law, should withdraw from the board and say, »I can't do my job like this!« (…) This is a mess from A to Z!« (A1, during interview)

Having met with several of Maucher's board members, this is, however, not the impression they give. The board members were strong personalities, not easily bullied, driven by the interest of Nestlé and willing to oppose the CEO should it be necessary. The impression was of a pro-active and intelligent board. It is true that not having received the study material well in advance may have hindered their process of opinion making as they could not have discussions with close colleagues, assistants and advisors, but rather ingested the information in isolation.

On the whole, however, considering the quality of the information provided by Maucher to the board members, it would appear that decisions could be reasonably made based on the material, and within this shorter time period for preparation. Inviting board members the previous night to study the material may therefore be more a question of Maucher's style and personal preference, rather than a ploy to destabilise his committee.

The anonymous interviewee had other contentions, however, believing that:

»Maucher hadn't the courage to bring people to the board who knew about Nestlé's business. Could he have? Yes. But he has not! Consciously, he hasn't brought in any food specialists and (…) if you don't understand anything about the business, then you can prepare for the meeting as long as you want, but you won't be able to talk shop! A board must answer honestly: do I understand the business or not? It's fine if not, then focus on the process. But both types are needed on the board.« (A1, during interview)

Maucher's opinion, however, that a board member does not necessarily need to be familiar with the business but rather be capable of asking the right questions, seems more pertinent. Maucher had strong personalities on his board, who were successful entrepreneurs and business leaders themselves.

The anonymous interviewee also claimed that no one objected to this *modus operandi* because »*everyone received 500k, and no one has had the courage*« (A1, during interview). It is interesting to note that de Weck also shared the opinion that money is an influencing factor. He once told a head-hunter conducting a study on the criteria for a director on a board that »*they have to be rich*« (Philippe de Weck, during interview). In other words, they must be wealthy enough to be independent and not reliant on the assignment. In the same vein, Hilb says:

»Never accept a board seat you can't afford to lose.« (Martin Hilb, during interview)

The idea that pay concerns hindered independence on Maucher's committee is not valid because most of Maucher's board members were wealthy and successful individuals and did not depend financially on this mandate.

Overall, the impression of the board is one of a strong culture in which members were critical and proactive: if the board did not get enough information, they would request it; if they were unsure, they would ask questions. Most significantly, the board asked the right questions, as described in the next chapters.

Acquisitions Within the Bounds of the Set Corporate Strategy

As CEO, Maucher only made acquisitions within the scope of the given strategy. The strategy was discussed in close co-operation with and approved by the board. In this way, the CEO did not make surprise acquisitions and any takeover was in line with the strategy. The board at Nestlé got involved once an acquisition exceeded a given amount, or if the acquisition was outside the mainline strategy.

As mentioned above, Maucher decided to impose a limit on his decision-making discretion because »*the competence of the CEO comes to an end once a certain acquisition size is reached*« (Helmut Maucher, during interview).

This is exemplary and reveals once again Maucher's carefully considered management approach which was a result of putting the interests of the company first. In spite of his strong personality, he recognised the importance of monitoring and feedback for a CEO and he instigated these additional checks and balances to make sure that the board agreed with and supported his decisions.

Maucher also sought board approval whenever he wanted to acquire a company that was outside the scope of Nestlé's strategy. Again he imposed limitations on himself and the board committee, declaring:

»The function of the board is to adjourn on important matters and determine a strategy beforehand. The CEO, or rather the committee, can act within these two parameters. You have to understand that otherwise you can't understand the nature of our business.« (Helmut Maucher, during interview)

Enhancing Market Presence through Acquisitions

Another goal of the company was to make acquisitions which were good prospects in the long-run and enhanced the Group's overall market presence within key nations and regions.

Carnation, an American manufacturer of food products from pet foods to milk, was one of the original takeovers in the sequence of acquisitions begun in 1984. It was a huge takeover then, equivalent to a »mega deal« now and it transformed Nestlé into a serious competitor in America, providing a great platform on which to build in the long run (Philippe de Weck, during interview).

Next came a series of acquisitions in a region where Nestlé had never been strong: Southern Europe was targeted in light of the fact that the European Single Market was beginning to form and the area was predicted to experience growth which was higher than average compare to the rest of Europe. This assumption was proved correct (Philippe de Weck, during interview).

Southern Asia, Egypt, several areas in China, and Eastern and Central Europe in particular were entered using takeovers by Nestlé. Moreover, Asia, a region which Nestlé felt had good potential in terms of development in the long run was the focus of acquisition, as was Latin America, in order to consolidate their place in the market there.

Reinforcing Product Groups through Acquisitions

Nestlé enhanced product groups through acquisitions and made business innovations and new business lines available to the Group.

In the majority of cases the form of Nestlé's acquisitions was horizontal and within its own industry. In this way, for example, Buitoni was acquired. It became obvious during this period, that in the future, people could not eat many kilos of meat per head annually, and a considerable portion of people's food intake would need to be derived from plants (like pasta).

Another canny acquisition was a host of long-standing mineral water firms, like Contrex, along with a robust franchise of springs in the U.S., which were acquired with Perrier. As Maucher said, »*When I started buying water people laughed at me – today they are not laughing*« (Helmut Maucher, during interview), and his board member, Bruno de Kalbermatten, confirmed Maucher's insightful thinking, »*It was quite trivial, but perfectly right, very bright!*« (Bruno de Kalbermatten, during interview).

In manufacturing premium water, supported by a global group with a degree of security, Nestlé was concentrating on strategic targets in the long run. Additionally, soft drinks were beginning to lose popularity for buyers watching their waists in nations which were industrialized, and this formed the foundation for the firm's water strategy. Nestlé became the number one supplier in the mineral water industry through acquiring Perrier.

Since then, Nestlé has sought to consolidate its place in the industry and increase growth through branding. Because the leading one or two product brands are more likely to sell or get innovations into shopping aisles, especially considering the growing concentration in the retail trade, retaining the top spot in a given market is even more vital now (Philippe de Weck, during interview). This same goal informed Nestlé's determination to make products stronger both in terms of market position and within the Nestlé Group as an entirety, whether within particular regions or nations.

For this reason, the Italian company making speciality confectionery and chocolate, Perugina, was acquired. Similar takeovers based on this principle were Chambourcy and Hirz, producing dairy products; the American firm Baby Ruth and Butterfinger; and Dalgety and Alpo, firms producing pet foods (Nestlé's first foray into the market was with Carnation) and ice-cream.

Creating Product Group Equilibrium through Acquisitions

When Maucher first came to the company, half of its profit was derived from Nescafé. He diagnosed this as »*nice but dangerous in the long term*«, recommending expansion of their product groups (Helmut Maucher, during interview).

Maucher also set about diversifying in terms of markets. As Maucher said, »*We can't make 50 percent of our profit in Europe in the long term, if the world grows in other places*« (Helmut Maucher, during interview). He therefore instigated a policy of investment in various countries including America and Asia.

Furthermore, he wanted these to be discussed and agreed on as the overall strategy together with the board, revealing how acquisitions solved these problems. Maucher began as he was set to continue, and the board's »*feedback was positive*« (Helmut Maucher, during interview).

Maucher clearly had a very firm grasp of the psychology of setting long- and short-term goals in profit and how they would be processed by interested parties. He persuaded the board to approve and invest in long-term goals because he made short-term profits:

»If I only promise long-term profits and make no profit in the short term then the public, the shareholders and the board become nervous. But people were satisfied with my work as the share value and profits kept on growing and with it productivity.« (Helmut Maucher, during interview)

Reducing the Timeframe for Top Market Positions through Acquisition

In several instances, as well as the need to ensure the business risk remained within controllable limits, the goal was to reduce the time needed to gain a top place in a vital segment of the market.

Rowntree, for instance, taken over in 1988 and headquartered in the U.K., contributed contemporary American-British concepts in confectionary and chocolate, especially Kit Kat. Without these takeovers, it would have been quite a high risk activity in a quickly changing market and, moreover, it would have taken years to reach this place in the market.

A shared venture with General Mills for breakfast cereals was embarked upon for similar reasons, to cut down the time necessary to ensure a powerful place in the market. Nestlé had a wary attitude to this, as with any fashionable movement. The Group tried to reach business goals through its own efforts, where feasible (Helmut Maucher, during interview), but on certain occasions, like in breakfast cereals, when the corporate culture was akin to their own, Nestlé did not dismiss shared ventures.

Financial Matters Related to Acquisitions

The importance of getting the correct price when acquiring companies, in terms of the firm's value as a whole, is another precondition for success.

Maucher's exceptional long-term vision is evident in his approach to the price of acquisitions. In his experience, *the most expensive acquisitions were the best and the cheapest often the worst* (Helmut Maucher, during interview). Maucher distinguished and was prepared to pay for what he felt had real value over the long term: *One often pays far beyond the book value, this is goodwill, but it is returned with long-term profitability* (Helmut Maucher, during interview).

One of Nestlé's board members, Bruno de Kalbermatten, elaborated on the difference between price and value. If the acquisition does not work out well, it is not so much a question of price as subsequent handling: *we need to know which parts to sell off and how to work with unions – redundancies, delocalisation of the production, etc.* (Bruno de Kalbermatten, during interview). Even Maucher's financial expert, Philippe de Weck, recognised this distinction: *I am a finance person myself, but the financial aspect comes last!* (Philippe de Weck, during interview).

At Nestlé, strategic considerations like brands or the value of distribution organisations and possible synergies (for example by marketing corresponding products through similar channels of distribution) are more important than the paper sums, when attempting to value a firm.

Moreover, when Maucher looked to the long term, he was not fazed by the financial analysts' dissuasions because an acquisition had a profit limitation of three years. In this instance Maucher would say to them:

Despite the fact that we only make a profit of X, it is a decision for a century. If we don't want to do that then we won't lead Nestlé, in the long term, to where we want to go. (Helmut Maucher, during interview)

Rowntree is a good example of this. The company paid more than CHF 6 billion for it. Maucher made sure that the additional interest was met by the additional profits, and that in terms of revenue, they would not be making a loss in the coming 2–3 years. Again he reiterated, *that was a decision for the century* (Helmut Maucher, during interview).

In terms of the confectionary industry, there were only two companies, Rowntree and Mars and *if we wanted to stay in chocolate, we had to do these acquisitions, and it proved worthwhile* (Helmut Maucher, during interview). Again, however, Maucher did not operate alone and asserted that:

The question of whether to operate in the long term or short term is very important and one that has to be discussed with the board as this is about strategy. (Helmut Maucher, during interview)

Clearly return in the long run is beneficial for the recently acquired firm and-or the group through the strategic benefits of acquiring the firm or the resultant synergies.

The initial year's profits, which ought at the very least to pay the interest on the supplementary loans needed, is a baseline condition.

As a result of changing competition or consumer attitudes, predictions are, in the longer term, frequently incorrect about the market economy. When a strategy that looks forward is used, there is increased time to get ready for integration as a whole and costs and the price of acquiring companies are usually not as big (Helmut Maucher, during interview).

When acquiring a firm, instigating a sequence of connected measures is another precondition for success. These involve putting businesses that make a loss up for sale in the case where losses, even in the long run, cannot be corrected, and getting rid of marginal activities to facilitate the focus on the core strengths and abilities of the group.

In line with the later policy, Nestlé got rid of the following, some of them of considerable size: hotel chains, the production of materials for packaging, Libby's preserves, Eurest, and several activities that were not, or were no longer in sync with their business strategy.

Taking on several fronts simultaneously was not an attractive prospect to Nestlé. Thus, other parts of the divestment plan included scrupulous cutbacks in overheads and costs that were fixed, streamlining production and product ranges, and flat organisations.

Stock Markets and Acquisitions

»I'm not against shareholder value but I'm against the powerful influence that it exerts, creating short-term thinking.« (Helmut Maucher, during interview)

The subject of financial markets and investor relations is something Maucher needed to consider in his position. He felt, however, that is was an aspect that was generally given too much weight. While admitting that it is particularly important for companies that are interested in returning to the capital market in terms of their capital costs and the exchange rate, his principle of prioritising the long term over the short term still held.

In this sense, Maucher criticised financial analysts: »I don't see how such a young financial analyst who just left university and has never seen a factory, can give me good advice!« (Helmut Maucher, during interview). He conceded that »in the short term their opinions are important, but over the long term it's *facts that matter«* because in his experience, *»a couple of years later the share price would increase because the market realised that the decision was right«* (Helmut Maucher, during interview). And indeed, his views were vindicated; during his headship, the market cap rose to over CHF 100 billion.

He was never concerned with what others feared in terms of diluted profits per share. While he took capital market reactions into account, he was not concerned by share price decreases because the company very rarely needed capital from the capital market. He felt that this was bad thinking, and if the *»board only thinks of their stock options they aren't acting in the interests of the company«* (Helmut Maucher, during interview). He knew anyway that the exchange rate, in the medium term, would remain stable and that if revenue and business experienced growth, it would be reflected in the market.

He did consider the capital market, however, in that he needed to be aware of the consequences and justify his longer-term strategies not only to himself and the board, but in an investor relations committee or conference. He thought he succeeded in bringing people around because *»in general (…) the share price always rose«* (Helmut Maucher, during interview).

He noted that he still had a duty to report on the markets to the board. The board regularly received information on the share price in comparison to competitors, and the Swiss Market Index. Furthermore, he would always report back on his visits to other markets when he went to investor relations conferences or came in contact with finance people and state representatives. Again, it was important to Maucher that *»the board is able to react«* and was *»completely informed of what was happening and also how the share capital was divided between the Americans and the Swiss«* (Helmut Maucher, during interview).

Soft Factors Contributing to the Nestlé Acquisitions Process

Effective Communication throughout an Acquisition

The communication and interaction between Maucher and the board was highly professional and intensive. Maucher ensured *»full transparency«* and that the board knew that it would be consulted about all major decisions *»anytime, immediately, the committee always knew what was happening«* (Helmut Maucher, during interview). He felt it vital to reach agreement between the board and committee on all fronts, however, *»one doesn't have to present the board with every little detail«* (Helmut Maucher, during interview).

Maucher's board members, such as Bruno de Kalbermatten confirmed this:

»We were always very informed. It was Maucher's idea to enter the chocolate market with Rowntree. I hesitated on this decision, but I understood that Nestlé wanted to get back into chocolate. Rowntree had a good image in England, so I said why not.« (Bruno de Kalbermatten, during interview)

According to Maucher too much information is produced which is often irrelevant and inaccurate. That which is pertinent is surprisingly little, for example, when Nestlé bought Carnation, it was the first big European acquisition of an American company.

The deal was USD 3.5 billion, which was a huge amount of money twenty years ago. Maucher »*handed exactly 13 pages to the board. These pages contained everything they needed to know and based on these thirteen pages, the board made its decision*« (Helmut Maucher, during interview).

This is how Maucher preferred to communicate with the board. It was not possible to get hold of any sources related to the Carnation acquisition, however, the following source shows the accuracy of Maucher's statement: a position paper addressed to the board from Maucher for the acquisition of Buitoni, constituting the same number of pages, thirteen in all.

Under examination, this document reflected again Maucher's precise and effective provision of relevant information for the board which ultimately allowed the board to make a decision based on sound information.

Maucher had this policy of brevity because he felt as a rule, details were not only irrelevant but often incorrect: »*the world moves differently to how people believe and an exaggerated, high number of studies feign a degree of exactness that doesn't exist at all*« (Helmut Maucher, during interview). His thirteen« pages contained everything he considered »*essential fundamentals*« which answered big questions like*:*

»Why are we going ahead with this acquisition? Are we making America stronger? Are we making pet food stronger? How much does it cost and how will we finance the project? That's all.« (Helmut Maucher, during interview)

By empowering the board with all of this information, he was also empowering himself: »*the position of the CEO is pretty strong. As long as he is successful the board will find it difficult to say ›no‹*« (Helmut Maucher, during interview). In this way he always obtained 100 percent agreement and had he »*misused their trust, they would have had the opportunity to react*« (Helmut Maucher, during interview).

Maucher's communication with the board was not only transparent, direct and pertinent but continued throughout the acquisition process as part of his reporting duty. Everything was reported: »*How will the project continue? How is the new acquisition going? Is it going well? Is it going badly? Does it comply with our plans? Are there problems?*« (Helmut Maucher, during interview). Furthermore, because decisions regarding acquisitions were not only about whether to buy or not, but also about ways of financing, other questions involved in the decision-making included: »*Do we take on new shares or are we doing it through commercial papers and trying to self-finance? Or do we take up a large, long-term loan?*« (Helmut Maucher, during interview).

The source below, »Dernier Developpements des Affaires Buitoni et Rowntree« of 3. 5. 1988, confirms this and is also proof of Maucher's continuous communication with the board in a brief, precise and effective manner (see Figure 2).

Effective Management of Social Aspects Which Result from Acquisitions

Moving to a new place, getting accustomed to another structure at their office, perhaps taking retirement or being made redundant are the consequences which M&A and restructuring processes have on individuals. It is important to bear in mind the individual's experience, despite the fact that many of the measures protect jobs in the long-run.

Alleviating the effects of a restructuring process, through a successful series of social measures, is clearly beneficial to a firm. According to Maucher, a programme like this is a fundamental precondition for an effective acquisition policy in the long-run (Helmut Maucher, during interview). Perception, drive and credibility are enforced by this means, according to Maucher, and money spent on this is just as vital as that spent on research or marketing.

The longevity of Nestlé's success is founded on trust, and in order to keep it, Nestlé must supply enough assistance to its personnel to adjust to new systems or secure alternative employment. From the outset, this has been a foundation stone of Nestlé's approach.

These days, when acquisitions or mergers are declared, executives tend to convey an attitude which is not balanced and sometimes, apparently, not very sophisticated: »*many people who carry out an acquisition, believe that they are the clever ones and the others are stupid*« (Helmut Maucher, during interview).

NESTLÉ S.A.

A Messieurs les membres
du Conseil d'administration
de NESTLE S.A.

Vevey, le 3 mai 1988

Messieurs,

Je me permets de vous faire part, ci-après, des derniers développements
des affaires Buitoni et Rowntree.

Buitoni

Un accord a finalement pu être conclu avec le groupe de Benedetti qui
permet de débloquer la situation en France : nous achèterons (indirec-
tement) à un prix forfaitaire de FF 1000.- par action 47% du capital de
Buitoni S.A. en France et nous disposerons d'une option pour 4% addi-
tionnels au même prix. Tout cela bien entendu sous réserve de l'accord
du Trésor français. Il est vrai que ce prix est d'environ FF 40.--
/action plus élevé que celui que nous aurions dû payer au groupe de
Benedetti selon le contrat original mais, par ce biais, nous serons en
mesure d'offrir un maintien de cours aux actionnaires minoritaires
français.

Notre intention est d'offrir aux actionnaires minoritaires un montant
en espèces de FF 1050.-- (ex dividende) par action. Ce prix est certes
élevé d'un point de vue strictement économique, mais nous avons dû
prendre en considération la situation actuelle en France en ce qui
concerne cette transaction qui est caractérisée, comme vous le savez,
par le refus des autorités boursières de Paris d'accepter la solution
proposée par M. de Benedetti, par la nomination d'un expert pour
défendre les droits des minoritaires, par des actionnaires (dont le
Crédit Agricole de France qui détient 10% du capital) qui, à tort ou à
raison, ont des expectations exagérées concernant la valeur de ces
actions etc. Tenant compte de la fourchette de FF 1100.-- à 1200.-- à
laquelle le marché s'attend à négocier ces titres, nous pensons

AVENUE NESTLÉ 55   CH-1800 VEVEY (SUISSE)   TÉLÉPHONE (021) 924 21 11   TÉLEX 451311 NES CH   TÉLÉFAX (021) 921 18 85   TÉLÉGRAMMES NESTLÉ VEVEY

*Figure 2: Helmut Maucher's Communication with the Board (»Developments
Regarding Buitoni and Rowntree«)*

néanmoins que le prix proposé nous permettra de réaliser cette affaire dans les meilleurs délais et de façon correcte et incontestable.

En ce qui concerne l'accord du Trésor, nous avons déjà entrepris tout ce qui était en notre pouvoir afin de l'obtenir dans les délais les plus courts.

Du point de vue financier, cette opération, incluant donc le 100% des actions de Buitoni France, coûtera au Groupe Nestlé env. Fr.s. 50 mio de plus que prévu dans les contrats de base. Le Comité du Conseil nous avait déjà accordé un montant limite de Fr.s. 80 mio pour nous permettre de débloquer la situation.

Rowntree

A la suite de nos conférences de presse de Londres et de Zurich, les réactions sont, à notre avis, aussi favorables que possible vu les circonstances. Nous pensons surtout que le message selon lequel notre intention est de poursuivre notre politique de ne pas faire d'OPA hostiles et que le cas de Rowntree revêt un caractère tout à fait exceptionnel qui, d'ailleurs, ne peut pas être qualifié de réellement hostile, a semble-t-il été compris. Nos démarches auprès des autorités et des membres du gouvernement ont jusqu'à maintenant trouvé un accueil normal. Rowntree a pu se rendre compte que seuls des arguments de nature politique et émotionnelle sont encore à leur disposition et ils en font un usage approprié. Un fait ressort très fréquemment dans les coupures de presse annexées : le manque de réciprocité; c'est-à-dire que les entreprises anglaises ne peuvent pas acheter des entreprises suisses car celles-ci sont protégées par l'enregistrement de leurs actions.

En ce qui concerne la bourse, nous avons pu, mardi 26.4.88, grâce à l'effet de surprise provoqué par l'annonce de notre offre publique d'achat, augmenter notre participation à 6,6%. Les premières minutes de surprise passées, le titre a atteint une cote au-dessus du niveau de notre offre, ce qui fait que nous n'avons plus pu acheter depuis. La plupart du volume est acheté en ce moment par Jacobs Suchard à un prix légèrement au-dessus de £ 9.- (nous avons annoncé un prix de £ 8.90 ex dividende, ce qui correspond à un prix effectif de £ 9.--/action). Jacobs Suchard a annoncé avoir atteint 23% hier soir et nous nous attendons à ce qu'il passe incessamment le cap des 25%.

Telle que se présente la situation aujourd'hui, ce serait, à notre sens, une erreur d'augmenter la valeur de l'offre maintenant, car Jacobs Suchard pourrait poursuivre ses achats à 15 p. au-dessus de notre offre. D'autre part, nous n'avons pour l'instant pas le sentiment qu'un autre acheteur important soit sur les rangs.

Figure 2: Next page

En l'absence d'une contre-offre par des tiers, Jacobs Suchard peut poursuivre pour le moment ses achats mais se verra contraint de les arrêter, au plus tard le jour où il atteindra le seuil des 30% puisqu'il sera alors dans l'obligation de faire une contre-offre. Selon toute vraisemblance, il devrait aller jusqu'à une participation d'environ 25%. Au moment où Jacobs Suchard (s'il ne veut pas faire de contre-offre) sera contraint de se retirer du marché et si, par surcroît, notre offre devait se heurter à des obstacles d'ordre politique ou autres, le cours du titre devrait baisser et nous pourrions recommencer à acheter.

Une bonne nouvelle vient de nous parvenir de Standard & Poor, à savoir que nous conserverons notre AAA-rating, même si les deux acquisitions Buitoni/Perugina et Rowntree étaient menées à bien.

Tout en me tenant à votre entière disposition au cas où des informations complémentaires vous seraient nécessaires, je vous prie de croire, Messieurs, en l'assurance de mes sentiments les meilleurs.

H. Maucher
Administrateur délégué

Figure 2: Next page

It was Maucher's policy, however, to listen because he did not believe that these people were stupid. He believed quite the opposite in fact. When Maucher bought the company Stouffer, its head became the head in America for a period. Later, when he bought Carnation and had to tell the head who was over seventy that he needed to leave, his successor not only became the head of Carnation but also the head in America. Maucher claimed that:

»I always made use of the most hard-working, able people. I've always told them: ›You belong to Nestlé, now you have the same opportunities as everyone else in our company!‹ I didn't only say it but also demonstrated it.« (Helmut Maucher, during interview)

Indeed, these psychological questions were critical to Maucher as he felt that they played a »*very crucial role regarding the eventual success of an acquisition*« through the »*leadership, motivation, and involvement of these people*« (Helmut Maucher, during interview).

It is interesting to note that Maucher changed his mind about hostile takeovers. At first, he was against them, but eventually came around to the idea that they were sometimes necessary; for example, Rowntree was a semi-hostile takeover. In this instance, Maucher revealed his people skills by going to the company immediately, by persuading them with sense, by motivating them and giving them opportunities. In this way they accepted the situation because Maucher »*operated clean policies and also created opportunities for new people. If it works out like that, people realise immediately that the takeover is a good thing*« (Helmut Maucher, during interview).

The need for transparency and communication grows gradually, particularly in larger firms, and communication on M&A ought to be perceived as a part of it. Maucher felt that a lot of acquisitions fail because of psychological mistakes, for instance, »*often whole ›field forces‹, are sent to the bought company, who think they know everything and cause frustration throughout the whole company*« (Helmut Maucher, during interview). Similarly, problems arise if the entire management are let go or the acquiring company's management are not involved enough. In this case, he felt »*a climate is created that leads to the situation where people are no longer motivated*« and this ultimately leads to failure (Helmut Maucher, during interview).

Maucher was very proud of the fact that Nestlé had »*never made any mistakes*« in this regard. He made sure to talk with the staff as well as the management, and »*kept managers who were capable in their positions or gave them the opportunity to find a new place within Nestlé*«. He dealt with the key players very carefully, however, because *»if they affected Nestlé in a bad way, then the company could fail«* (Helmut Maucher, during interview).

Another consideration is that of the long- and short-term view; when merging, companies frequently put too much emphasis on an immediate and positive stock market response. Thus, Maucher reported, some companies that Nestlé took on were *»allowed to operate cautiously for a while with the aim of integrating them gradually«* (Helmut Maucher, during interview). Synergies were something Nestlé was aiming for from the very beginning, but integration took place step-by-step: *»all these are steps where one can make mistakes or actually get it right«* (Helmut Maucher, during interview).

As an example of this, for a long time Maucher had two heads in America who reported to him directly. While they worked together, synergies were always slow in coming. So when a financial analyst asked Maucher why he didn't merge the two posts, he said, *»because I'm cleverer than you«* (Helmut Maucher, during interview). By operating like this, the firms functioned well and made profits. Then later, once they had become used to each other, having only one head became possible (Helmut Maucher, during interview).

Maucher cited several releases in the press, which, after a merger or acquisition, were connecting increased profits in the billions, to decreased staff numbers. That profits would increase and more jobs would be ensured in the long run would perhaps have been a more constructive way of conveying these mergers, as a vital strategic move for the firm.

Sourcing outside the firm might also be considered in this matter since, in practice, a lot of immediate cutbacks in employment are, in fact, only transference of these jobs to smaller firms. Shareholders are not the only party with interest in large mergers and acquisitions, and it is vital to develop an appropriate and balanced communication between all the parties concerned.

One way of looking at it is that in order to ensure the long-lasting life of a firm, the pain of a merger must be endured. Furthermore, a rise in profits will mean money can be spent on greater development of the business and assist alleviation of the social impact of mergers and acquisitions (in Europe and Switzerland the payout ratio in companies is normally extremely low).

The enhanced effectiveness of the company in the long run rather than the short term was the aim of an acquisition or merger for Nestlé.

Communication with Stakeholders during an Acquisition

Maucher strongly believed that the board has nothing to do with the duty to communicate with the target company during the acquisition process or more broadly with shareholders, press, analysts, interest groups and other stakeholders. This is the CEO's role as he is closest to the business, runs it and has an advantage in terms of information and experience. The board, however, must be informed and support decisions and their communication.

Nestlé's Attention to Post-merger Integration

Awareness of the importance of the integration process was not only present at management level under Maucher, but at the same time at board level. According to Bruno de Kalbermatten, the board were always asking questions related to the subject of integration and if it *»was happening harmoniously, or if there was something blocking it«* (Bruno de Kalbermatten, during interview). Rowntree, for example, *»was a family business, they were all rich, there wasn't much happening in the company anymore… that's when they started to be afraid. When we arrived, I think it made them happy«* (Bruno de Kalbermatten, during interview).

In terms of coping with the integration of a newly acquired firm, Nestlé fully respected Drucker's principles. Furthermore, besides providing equal opportunities to all personnel, Nestlé stressed the importance of working alongside the acquired firm's management. They were also extremely cautious of implementing the Group's approach harshly.

4.4.4 Conclusion on Nestlé's Strategy in Acquisition

»We've always said that we want to run businesses that we understand. So we want to practice authentic business leadership. Therefore it is forbidden to acquire things that don't suit us.« (Helmut Maucher, during interview)

Indeed, his board members reiterated this fact in several interviews:

»My policy has always been, even in my own company, to do what we can do best, to improve it, and not to go into something else; don't enter a technology field you don' t understand.« (Bruno de Kalbermatten, during interview)

A clearly outlined merger and acquisition policy was created and installed by Nestlé; the acquired firms needed to fall inside Nestlé's own industry experience and be of significance to the Group. The new companies should also be reciprocally improving and promoting synergies through new activities. The Group's enhanced product range or presence in certain nations was a vital part of the mergers and acquisitions.

Favouring mutual consent and discussion, the Group did not deem hostile bids acceptable. The firm mostly chose innovative companies with expertise that the Group did not have which were small or medium in size.

Though market share did affect Nestlé's choice of acquisitions in several instances it was not the sole consideration. Particularly when Nestlé aimed to become the leader in the market, costs were a vital consideration when acquiring companies.

Essentially, five key elements provided the basis for the Group's strategy on M&A:

Firstly, a readiness to benefit from each other's knowledge was necessary. The Group understood that the mixture of personnel's experience and knowledge was one of the main reasons for the effectiveness of their M&A. Consequently, a readiness to impart knowledge was also essential in personnel.

Secondly, the Group brought its strengths to all of its acquisitions, enhancing aspects such as their place in the market, product range, and structure of management.

Thirdly, on the whole, firms where the basic elements were not strong were not acquired by the Group. Those that were taken over needed to have good prospects for growth in the longer run as well as technology and marketing expertise.

Fourthly, in terms of processes and market, the Group limited M&A to areas which were connected to their current or recently acquired experience or range of products.

Finally, the Group did not want to end up as a widely diversified corporation nor did it reach towards acquisition of Nestlé's supply chain or the expansion of products, for example, in the manufacturing of raw materials, and/or services to related areas in order to more directly fulfil customer's needs.

In the interviews with Nestlé board members and the chief executive, it was clear that Nestlé followed long-term strategies.

Maucher explained that most discussions on the topic of shareholder value were about short-term or long-term aspects (Helmut Maucher, during interview). But »*as soon a shareholder is willing to think like me about what is good for the long term I'm likely to agree with him 95–100 percent.«* (Helmut Maucher, during interview).

Maucher further explained that in social policies, too, the management can solve almost anything if it thinks in the long term:

»In the long term we're all in the same boat. If you want to maximize in the short term then you let 6000 people go and as a result don't have an optimized business and no motivation. Therefore I'm all for investing with the social factor in mind in order to avoid much bigger damage.« (Helmut Maucher, during interview)

Maucher believed that if the management thinks longer-term and is more interested in staff motivation, company image, longer-term revenue security, *»then many conflicts disappear that emerge in the short term«* (Helmut Maucher, during interview).

For such a long-term view a true leader needs strength and the nerve to withstand criticism, two characteristics that Maucher clearly conveyed:

»I always say personality is almost more important than anything else. Bosses who don't have character, who don't have a brass neck and who don't possess communication skills to persuade others will have a hard time.« (Helmut Maucher, during interview)

Maucher was convinced that the main cause of failure was a bad CEO:

»You can't have people in this position who are too vain, get carried away, or become obsessed with power. They need to exercise their power because that is part of their job but if these people become irrational then they are in the wrong place.« (Helmut Maucher, during interview)

Maucher believed that for an acquisition to be a success, the board's crucial role was not increased involvement, but simply hiring the right CEO. Maucher continued:

»Saying' that's a nice guy, I'll let him get on with things and give him an efficient assistant'. Wrong. You never can solve a problem from the bottom up. A bad CEO needs to go. The higher the position the more important the change.« (Helmut Maucher, during interview)

Further to this, Maucher felt that while officially, the board would always have greater power, in reality, the board relied much more on the CEO. For this reason he was against the expression »ultimate responsibility« (»Oberleitung«), which was brought into Switzerland by Mr. Boeckli:

»Even today no one really knows what that means. I don't care about this term as long as the board has the opportunity to delegate its main leadership 90 percent to the CEO.« (Helmut Maucher, during interview)

It is also important to note that while external growth through acquisitions was key to the developments that Maucher led, he was always aware of the importance of organic growth: »*the latter needs to be a given, otherwise the company loses its dynamic*« (Helmut Maucher, during interview).

Maucher made two-thirds of Nestlé's profit through acquisitions and one third through internal growth and in this way he put the company, in a short period of time, into a new position. Indeed, he was ahead of his contemporaries:

»I had to do that before everyone else realised what globalization meant or what water meant, or what pet food meant. I shortened the process. Ten years later everything« would have become much more expensive« (Helmut Maucher, during interview).

Thus, a powerful, original mind was at work, capable of measuring the needs of different parties, exploiting their strengths in an incisive and effective manner, creating systems that were new and inventive, and perhaps, most significantly recognising the need for constructive relationships without ego.

4.5 Worst Case Scenario: Swissair

»I wasn't on the Swissair board. I have talked to people from an outside point of view and saw more than the board members. That's what I really felt. It's a tragedy that one can trace back to human mistakes. It is regrettable and it hurt me for Switzerland. (…) I believe they were partly befuddled and partly Mr. Bruggisser didn't inform them accurately. For me it's hardly comprehensible how sensible and reasonable people, who are in fact good, could watch for such a long time. This can only be board befuddlement (…) and weakness (…) I still don't understand it (…) For me it's a phenomenon. But I can't explain it any differently.« (Helmut Maucher, during interview)

In the Nestlé case, many key players on the board were willing to provide rich and detailed information on the interaction of the board and management during acquisitions. Documentation was necessary only to confirm the facts, which were all agreed upon amongst the members, and were further augmented with observation. Individual exploration of the acquisition cases was therefore not considered particularly fruitful or necessary.

For Swissair, however, I had difficulties in organising interviews and many requests for meetings were declined, to a large degree because of ongoing legal claims against board members. Those who did agree to meet were reluctant to give information, or not close enough to the TMT to have insight into the relationship between the board and management. As a result, there is greater emphasis in the following on the hard facts of the individual acquisitions, in an attempt to deduce motives and relationships.

As a note on terminology: SAirlines refers to the airline section of Swissair which was itself one part of Swissair Group which became SAirGroup in 1997. Reasons for the collapse of the firm can be discovered in the very complicated circumstances of the company and soft factors.

Clearly, the TMT of the company were significantly affected emotionally through processes of denial, the desire to hold on, identification and attachment. The case continues to have an important emblematic significance. An in-depth examination of the social relations that occurred inside the top leadership parties, along with gaining complete knowledge of meeting etiquette and so on, would be the only method of carrying out an absolutely scientific examination of the firm's top leadership and how they precipitated the decline of the firm.

The time frame 1992–2001 is examined as this covers the period when the company's worsening situation began spiralling towards its end in 2001. In this book, chosen texts on the case are carefully examined and conclusions are based on material like the annual reports.

In October 2001, Swissair entered into receivership and the chosen liquidator ordered a report. In spring of that same year, the general convention asked for a special enquiry into the top management employee shuffles, the Hunter Strategy and the resultant and unprecedented loss of almost CHF 3 billion in the business year of 2000. This happened previous to receivership. Ernst & Young (E&Y) was brought in to conduct a special examination of the case during the summer of 2001, and in particular to answer a host of queries generated by the judge and shareholders which would be used in deciding degrees of responsibility in the eyes of the law.

4.5.1 Critical Remarks on the E&Y Report

It is important to mention several aspects of the report prior to moving into a full scale discussion with the aid of the qualitative information sourced. It should be noted that E&Y inevitably examined the information and its context from a particular perspective: »*That this does not contain the declarations and opinions of the relevant individuals is the most negative aspect of the document*« (Vollentweiler, during interview).

Indeed, this misgiving was mentioned by other interviewees as well. The value of one-on-one discussion was revealed by conducting interviews. Thus the document would have been improved by adding a sizable and broad portion of the views and elucidations of the various individuals. It is therefore important to look at the report bearing in mind that it does not fully represent the events but rather is one of several illuminating and partial sources.

It is also important to note that, as a result of the examination's remit, the report focused mainly on negative aspects. Though the document attests to portraying events with a factual objectivity, it clearly does not live up to this by virtue of its distinctly negative flavour. Once more, the temptation to see events in a negative light is strong. In fact, other European carriers aspired to being like Swissair for a long time as it had many successes to its name, not least in terms of its place in the national identity (Probst & Mercier 1992). It is worth remembering this.

4.5.2 Description of the Firm

In the early 1930s, the company was formed through the merger of Ad Astra and Balair (Probst & Mercier 1992). Over the following seventy years, within a market which became progressively tougher, the company grew with ground-breaking courage and determination. The company got bigger through keeping up with the forefront of aircraft equipment advances and by constantly offering top-class services and products.

In this way, the airline always aimed to operate in a global market. This would have been enough to get on in prosperous periods and subsist in downturns, as long as the government took care of landing rights, ensured prices were high and constant and the market was controlled by inhibiting competitors. However, in an uncontrolled market, coupled with very strong competitors, the company had to discover new competitive means, as discussed in the following chapter.

As an emblem of promptness, dependability, top-end service and financial success, Swissair was, for Switzerland, a part of the cultural identity and a secure staple. This is a vital to understand.

Until the beginning of the liberalisation of the airlines in Europe in the late 1980s and the global cessation of nations' sole control, rights to land had been regulated by agreements between nations which limited capacities and rights. Particularly for the airlines which were not as big and operated in a domestic context, things altered significantly at the start of the 1990s as they began to take effect. This time of deregulation resulted in loss of profits for numerous airline companies in Europe (E&Y 2003/1, p. 1).

When Switzerland voted no in 1992 to the referendum on joining the EU, Swissair was at a strategic disadvantage because the company would still have to negotiate European landing rights where its EU counterparts could enjoy an open market (NZZ 2001/6). Furthermore, to avoid losing its licence to operate, the company was only permitted to take shares of less than 50 percent in airlines in Europe (E&Y 2003/1, p. 2)

Strategically, the firm could go forward through the formation of partnerships in Europe (whether based on buying shares or not) in order to become a good partner choice for a bigger firm (e.g. Delta-Airlines), or Swissair could become part of a bigger system (e.g. British Airways) (E&Y 2003/1, p. 2).

The Hunter Strategy was put in place in reaction to Switzerland's vote on the EU agreements so as to bypass discussions with every single EU member on rights to land.

Between 1992–2001, the years of serious decline, many attempts were made to save the company: the Alcazar Project did not succeed in conjoining the firm with Austrian Airlines, Royal Dutch Airlines and Scandinavian Airlines; and similarly, the Hunter Strategy did not succeed in installing Swissair as leader of a group of state flag airlines because it was, strategically, too risky and costly. These failed attempts were a result of a multitude of different causes where no single event or individual was solely responsible.

In this corporate governance examination there is particular focus on the acquisition period of the Hunter Strategy covering 1997–2001. Various sources, along with E&Y, report in detail on the many companies acquired including the interactions and dealings of the top management during this period. Actions during the Hunter Strategy period give a very good idea of the wider top management and board team's *modus operandi* (or lack thereof) at the time, although there are a number of contributing causes in the collapse of the company.

4.5.3 Corporate Governance Structure and Its Weaknesses

Board-Management Relationship

As illustrated, literature generally states that it is the duty of the board of directors to create the strategic orientation of the firm. As it will be shown, because of industrial deregulations and the resultant increase in competition, this was a difficult task in Swissair. As will be discussed, the company attempted to deal with these new challenges in a newly opened market by means of several strategies involving acquisitions.

As will be seen, there was a dramatic swing from a scenario in which the board completely dominated the CEO to one in which the CEO acted without meaningful or effective board involvement. In both instances there was a lack of cooperation in terms of the strategic orientation.

The board-management relationship was ineffective. As will be illustrated, the board did not receive sufficient information. In a press article, chairman Honegger revealed that Swissair's board directors were not able to check the financial situation of all the targets before they were acquired. He reported that instead the board had to rely on the due diligence of the CEO, his team and different consultancy firms (NZZ 2001/2).

This is a valid point, but after perusing in detail the due diligence reports, the board's duty was to pose vital, effective questions. Rather than doing this, the Swissair board assumed without question that CEO Bruggisser and Schorderet, his CFO, were reliable in terms of both the firms acquired and the Group's financial reports. In 1998, the Group showed decent financial statements to the public which did not suggest signs of problems.

Later, the issues were clear but only to an expert in accounting. Complex agreements involving various options accompanied many of the acquisitions, and in spite of the quantity of information made available to the public, the fact that these partner firms were in trouble was not apparent. The Group did not own more than 50 percent in the majority of these firms, and full consolidation was unnecessary (NZZ 2001/3).

Indeed, Hostettler, a consultant in HR management and remuneration, confirmed this in his interview:

»I think we've measured performance incorrectly for a long time. I've no idea why the share price continues to go up. I think had the participations been properly consolidated at an earlier stage, if EVA had been measured, etc, if you really pulled through the economic perspective and were not so concerned with revenues and turnover, then it probably would have been recognised earlier what was going on.« (Stephan Hostettler, during interview)

Malik states that a firm's position in terms of strategy is not apparent in accounting numbers, as the intermittently healthy financial figures reveal (Malik 2001, p. 27). It should be noted here that PWC, Swissair's auditor, attested to the accuracy of their bookkeeping (NZZ 2001/4). The board ought to have assessed and controlled the finances more closely particularly in light of the complexities of the Group and the various financial and strategic warnings should have instigated greater involvement from the Swissair board of directors in terms of assessment and control of the performance. An obvious signal, for instance, that the board's strategy was not aligned to the market was the fact that crucial partners like Austrian Airline, Singapore and Delta dropped out.

The Board

For the analysed period, I examined the annual reports as a general indication of the board. In all, there were approximately sixty members during this period, a comparatively large number of people. Only around seven members made up the committee of the board. It is pertinent to note the quantity of individuals on the board, regular members, who did not have a direct role.

In terms of the background of individual board members, there was an appreciably high volume of individuals from political circles in Switzerland and those belonging to important Swiss businesses. Influential foreign members also began appearing in the 1999 annual report. Furthermore, state representatives from federal and local levels as well as representatives from regions and major cities were involved at all times as were individuals from large-scale Swiss industrial firms and financial services. Clearly the health of the Swiss flag bearer was important to all of these members and those they represented.

Authors like Hilb recommend composition based on thorough consideration of the individual's skills. This does not appear to be the case in Swissair. Rather, it would appear from the documents examined, that the hiring process, under the chairperson and current members, was used to induct important political or business people in Switzerland. Until 2000, the »old« committee did not seem to have a structure with positions that required particular skills, but when the new structure was ushered in, it is likely that some sort of underlying principles based on contemporary business practices were used for choosing new members.

The Swiss have a comparatively small network of businesses because of the militia-system in which Swiss individuals are allowed to stand in several military, political and business positions« at once, creating small business circles and networks. Numerous people contend that new executives are difficult to source as it is a small nation and this is the reason for the leaders holding several roles simultaneously. It is worth noting, however, that legally a stock firm's board of directors must constitute a majority Swiss membership (Art. 708 OR).

The chairman was a full time job in Swissair, where the rest of the board carried out their particular jobs alongside other responsibilities. It is interesting to note that none of them had previous airline experience.

It is certain that all board members held at least one other time-consuming and demanding office; for instance, Honegger, as full-time head of the Group was on the NZZ and UBS board of directors as well. It is unclear, however, with what effectiveness the Swissair board met. It is stated in the annual report from 1993 that the committee, pre-restructuring, met twelve times at frequent intervals that year (Swissair 1994, p. 9).

Board Committees

A board committee comprising vice-presidents, a few other members and a president was created because of Swissair's large board of directors. In 1999, the committee was made the »nucleus« board of directors. Three committees which were not as big were also created in this new structure, covering compensation, finances and organisational matters (Swissair 2000, p. 52). No sources are accessible in terms of the exact duties and *modus operandi* of these committees.

It is important to note that an advisory board was also created in the same year during this restructuring of the board, comprising several new and old players. Important figures like the former financial minister of Germany, Theo Waigel, were involved in this board. As far as can be ascertained, there are no sources of information on the efficacy of this advising body, and it must be presumed that they had very little or no influence on the choices made subsequently. Again, it would appear that membership of the Group's board was more of an honorific title than a position associated with significant duties.

Board Culture

To some extent the Group's culture was characteristic of corporate culture in Switzerland, in that it was based on a community in which those coming from the exterior are initiated into the »circle« previous to being given responsibilities. This pattern can be seen as representative of the behaviour of the Group's board previous to the big changes after 2000. The board was fairly fixed during this earlier period, with a nucleus of prominent individuals.

It would appear that the Group's board culture was perceptibly influenced by the composition and structure of the board of directors, in that it was mainly based on the influence and reputation of national and business concerns in Switzerland. In the Swissair Group, the division of supervisory duties and those of management was not appropriately maintained as is recommended for a firm's structure. It is safe to presume further that there were various types of board culture in Swissair due to the large numbers on the board. There was also a variety of skills and backgrounds present. Furthermore, members who were younger and more active, like Lukas Muehlemann, were assumed to be more crucial than others and even the president.

Bruggisser and Loepfe's inclination to evolve controversial strategies covertly, away from the board from the outset and without their vital input, must be viewed as a result of there being a big board in terms of numbers whose prestigious political and business members had their own concerns. This behaviour betrays a serious problem in the culture, generated by the very large body of the board of directors.

A widespread issue in the literature is a board's closely knit business circles. It is a good thing in that such small business circles lead to greater efficacy in a business environment which is progressively more cooperative; however, it is a bad thing when the interest of an individual leads to differences between members. These business networks become bad things when the open culture, within and without, is lost. In other words, a mentality is created within the group which rejects objections from within the group and defends against those from the exterior, thus disabling external collaboration (NZZ 2002).

Another cause of cultural insufficiency may be that the directors endorsed the management's strategic plans. It is worth bearing in mind that strategic matters and surrounding factors were becoming more complicated. It is unlikely that board directors would admit that their comprehension was incomplete, that they had drifted from being able to see the bigger perspective, or that they no longer agreed with a strategy that they had previously endorsed.

It would appear that a constructive and open culture is necessary when adaptability is needed in the face of complications. In this case, the board was unable to bring together its collective knowledge and experience to operate as a strong unit because the team was constituted for reasons of reputation and operated to avoid intervention.

Thus, its power seemed to have been diminished to the lowest common denominator and the board's inefficiency was largely a result of the lack of communication between members themselves and between top management and the board. Macus' suggestion that the board's lack of success was a result of inefficient board interactions rather than poor board composition or structure, is borne out under this analysis (Macus 2002).

For example, while the individuals in the Group were not depicted in the E&Y report, various statements were suggestive of their character. The report revealed that Bruggisser regularly attended and was outspoken at meetings of the board, and thus was clearly a vital player. He appeared to possess great self-assurance and a forthright character. Indeed, in the final stages, he appears to have disobeyed the board's directives, suggesting an ambitious, unbending and perhaps a rather egotistical personality. As Maucher commented during interview, Bruggisser was forceful in pushing his strategy through and would only share his plans when it suited him (Helmut Maucher, during interview).

George Schorderet, the CFO, was usually quiet at these meetings, but he was outspoken at the meetings of the financial commission, at which Bruggisser was not attendant. This suggests loyalty to his superior, Bruggisser, and unwillingness to conflict with his opinions.

Honegger was severely criticised in the E&Y report. There was a great sense, however, that Honegger was out of his depth and took a long time to make choices because he was waiting for Bruggisser to give an opinion first. A suggestion of his doubt lies in the fact that he did not insist that the board's directives given to Bruggisser were followed, and it seems beyond question that Bruggisser had the stronger character.

4.5.4 M&A Strategy: An Integral Failure

In order to remain competitive the company made eight acquisitions of airlines in Europe in 1995 and during the period 1998–2000. The expansion was hindered, however, by the fact that the majority of the acquisitions were in financial difficulties. Thus, quite apart from the cost of acquiring the airlines, means had to be made available to restructure them.

These transactions happened very quickly without due consideration of their financing. A coherent vision was not in place as the board's finance committee did not agree with these purchases. If due diligences were made, the suggestions made during the discussion and by the board were subsequently ignored. Founded mostly on the overly confident projections about resultant synergies, more money was spent on these acquisitions than they were actually worth. The practices of the financial manual were not adhered to in terms of the proposals made to the board and companies were acquired without any consideration for the lack of financial awareness about them.

Furthermore, frequently, the expected investment figure was hugely overreached resulting in an overall spend of almost CHF 6 billion on the acquired firms, loan and guarantee claims, and share firms. The consequence of this dearth in assessment and control of finances was a loss of liquidity, worsened by Swissair's ignorance or decision to ignore the difficult dynamics outside the firm which were beyond its control. Eventually, by way of a chain of events, choices were made on various occasions which were incorrect and dynamics outside the firm developed which could not have been predicted, but resulted in insolvency.

The Alcazar, Sabena and Hunter Strategy constitute three eras of key directional changes in the Group's corporate journey.

Overview of Strategies: Alcazar, Sabena and Hunter

An Opportunity Not Seized: the Alcazar Project

The Alcazar Project was a key scheme of the early 90s propelled by the energies of Loepfe, the chief executive, as were numerous other strategies. Its ultimate aim was to merge Royal Dutch Airlines, Scandinavian Airlines, Austrian Airlines and SAirGroup. The chief executives wanted to create a group that would be a powerful body in Europe's airline industry alongside Lufthansa, Air France and BA. Growing difficulties with the ever bigger numbers of stakeholders stunted the initial optimism in the talks.

The bad result from these discussions, and the final downfall of the scheme, were a consequence of several things: *firstly*, the talks caused antagonism in the relevant firms' own nations as it was impossible to keep the plans under wraps; and *secondly*, the individual firms were primarily concerned with their own stakeholders' interests.

Similarly, SAirGroup was unwilling to make concessions regarding its own stakeholders' interests or indeed, those of the firm, according to their 1993 annual report (Swissair 1994, p. 4). Since SAirGroup was considered the most powerful of all the firms involved, it was thought in the national press that by merging they would lose out in the end (Luechinger 2001). Because of this, the negotiating team from Swissair were alienated due to a growing sense of self-importance. The record reports that lack of agreement from the U.S. partner caused the failure of the talks. Whatever the case, the top management at SAirGroup were stranded with no direction.

The talks included the boards of directors from the outset. As part of the negotiations, the president, Goetz, as well as the managers in the company had demanded well-paid offices in the new Group. Indeed, Goetz was earmarked for president of the Group due to his high rank and Swissair's clout in the talks (Luechinger 2001, pp. 138).

It could be contended that the board were too subjective to grasp the significance of the transaction for Swissair, in the sense that they were defending their own business and political interests in the national carrier. Without doubt, Alcazar was not a success in the end because of unwillingness to compromise and hot-headedness.

A Portentous Project: Sabena Airlines

Talks with Sabena Airlines, the Belgian flag bearer, began not long after the unsuccessful Alcazar talks. A letter of intent was signed with Sabena during the summer of 1994 and Swissair finally bought a 49 percent share in the company in the following year (Swissair 1996, p. 5). In the same year, McKinsey & Company suggested three possible courses of action after assessing the value of the stake in Sabena: they could merge with a large airline, create a network through an assertive acquisition policy, or remain independent.

Bruggisser, Muehlemann and McKinsey became increasingly influential players the more complicated the circumstances and strategy became. The board turned into a less influential force. The board's supposed experience was greatly overshadowed by that of extremely skilled global managers under Bruggisser.

At the outset, Bruggisser was very suspicious of the Sabena Project, and the choice to invest was made by Goetz and Loepfe, the previous chief executive (NZZ 2001/7). Indeed, Swissair's head of HR, Moelleney, reported that »*the board viewed themselves as the strategy-makers and insisted the CEO carried them out, or he would be replaced*« (Moelleney, during interview). Subsequently, according to Moelleney:

»Bruggisser then implemented the strategy – growth through acquisition deals – and came into his own. He took charge and said ›ok then, I'll do that, but now I make the strategy and I take matters into my own hands and I don't let the board dictate to me what to do‹.« (Matthias Moelleney, during interview)

Other interviewees, including, a Swissair board member, confirmed the above view (Anonymous, during interview).

Bringing the full amount to 85 percent, the board endorsed another acquisition of shares in Sabena in April 2000. Despite the detrimental financial consequences for Swissair due to the fact that Sabena Airlines did not have a positive equity-to-debt ratio, and once more, with no papers on it, this was carried out. Furthermore, this was implemented contrary to the firm's overarching strategic view of the moment (E&Y 2003/2, p. 21). Resulting in bad media attention in Belgium, the SAirGroup withdrew from its agreements with Sabena Airlines at a later point.

The aim of this acquisition was to begincreating a carrier group headed by Swissair. There were no written resources but rather a slide show formed the basis of the decision making process for the board of directors alongside an oral proposal. As a result, there was little comprehension and they grossly undervalued the finances necessary to sustain Sabena.

There was apparently no vision, in terms of strategy, during this process of acquisition which was carried out in the interval between the Alcazar Project and the Hunter Strategy. Buying long haul planes and maintaining routes that were not helping to develop the firm was one of the major mistakes. Throughout, the firm appeared to have a muddled approach to Sabena: Sabena might have evolved to relate as a feeder to Swissair and might have operated successfully as a regional airline.

Overly Ambitious: the Hunter Strategy

Context of the Strategy
In the wider exploration of Swissair's acquired companies there is particular concentration on the Hunter Strategy. The reason for this is that E&Y supply in-depth information on this period. They also depict the interactions between the board and management and this is useful, because in compari-

son to the Nestlé case study, the empirical interview material is limited for Swissair.

The Hunter Strategy was a result of Switzerland's refusal to partake in the EEC's agreement opening up access to the markets of Europe in 1992. The strategy aimed to bypass individual bilateral talks with each EEC member on rights to land. Due to space restrictions and the projected capacity thresholds in Central and Northern Europe, there were more opportunities for greater capacity of the main airports of Eastern and Southern Europe; the potential to bring customers to SAirGroup by way of partnerships; the projected benefits in terms of competition and synergies as a result of the partnerships; and the possibility of Europe having greater transcontinental air travel alongside Germany, Britain and France (E&Y 2003/1, p. 12). The Hunter Strategy was hence founded on these projections of how the airline business might evolve.

The primary aim was to enlarge and control the Swiss market by way of clever partnerships with home airlines whose economies were developing. By way of smart timing of flights and airport connections, business could be expanded at a number of airports which had possibilities for growth. The goal was the eventual alliance with a larger company, thereby retaining autonomy. In order to achieve this, in early 1998 the firm's board decided to make their position in the Swiss market stronger.

The secondary aim was to make greater forays into the mature (or »third«) markets, whose national flag bearers were powerful players but were restricted in the longer term by capacity, such as the French, Italian, German, and British carriers, and thereby reap the benefits of synergies within the expanded Swissair Group (E&Y 2003/1, p. 13–15). In this way, they could redirect customers through the company's centre of transcontinental travel, Zurich (E&Y 2003/1, p. 52). These were the vital components in becoming a viable partner to an international group.

In spite of initial plans, the strategy was not followed. The aim of expanding their own market was only fulfilled when the firm acquired the national carrier of Poland, LOT. The firm made acquisitions in mature markets in every instance besides this, which was not in line with the initial plan (E&Y 2003/1, p. 53).

Furthermore, with an estimated capital outlay of approximately CHF 300 million, gaining less than 50 percent of shares in chosen partner carriers was part of the original Hunter Strategy . In fact, expanding greatly on this plan, the maximum amount of shares (49 percent permitted by EU regulation) was frequently acquired. On occasion, by way of complicated and precarious financial agreements, the firm sometimes ended up with total financially responsibility. Indeed, at times, these were risky acquisitions, with a value of up to CHF 4.2 billion, which involved placing options on purchases in the future (E&Y 2003/1, pp. 54). These actions resulted in a fourth European alliance in 1998 called Qualiflyer, but Delta, Austrian and Singapore Airlines, the major players in it, left due to strategic reasons.

Engineering and Approval of the Strategy

In the final months of 1997, Bruggisser, the chief executive of the firm, brought in the consulting experts McKinsey & Company in order to help evolve the Hunter Strategy. In the following months, because of the contentious circumstances, a group was created to evolve and frame the strategy to address the difficult issues. It consisted of a few high level managers, consulting experts from outside the firm and Bruggisser (E&Y 2003/1, p. 18).

As a result of the first and a second meeting, and with great speed, the strategy was approved in January 1998 by the TMT and three days later by the board committee.

In terms of the approval by the committee of the board and by the management team, there is no proof that the financial overview documents, or even the strategy document on the risks of synergies and the potential financial consequences, were supplied to them.

Both of these overviews revealed that as the strategy unfolded, there would be an unavoidable increase in the costs in terms of capital, and also that the acquisition airlines which Swissair aimed at had experienced, in the period 1988–1997, an almost CHF 2.5 billion loss (E&Y 2003/1, p. 20).

Despite the fact that the board did not have proven participation in the project or its operations as per procedure, they ought to have been monitoring its evolution. It also appears that, previous to the mentioned approval date, several individuals on the board had not seen any paper to do with the strategy.

That Bruggisser was the driving force during the creation of the project and its approval is the deduction reached in the section on the TMT in the E&Y report (E&Y 2003/1, p. 19). In spite of the regulations and principles surrounding strategy as outlined in Swiss law and in the role of the board team, and despite the fact that the firm had a full time board president, no proof exists that the board team took part in these events during this period.

Furthermore, in January 1998, consent was officially granted for the strategy by the committee of the board, who had not had a role in its preparation; in fact, they approved it on the very day they first came across it.

EXECUTION OF THE STRATEGY

»Everyone who knows about board management realises that the board should not buy third and fourth class companies. You do not even have to be on the board to be able to see that. Also, a phenomenon that no one realised was that during these events they also had to cover for some of the targets' liabilities – and look at the trade unions in France.« (Arthur Loepfe, during interview)

On three separate occasions throughout the execution of the Hunter Strategy, McKinsey had told Bruggisser of the potential dangers of it.

By way of the means below, the directors of the board might have ensured they were up to date with information:

In the annual business strategy document, the co-dependencies within the group were not sufficiently demarcated as this document reviews all levels of the sections within a timeframe of three years. They also failed to quantify the extra funds and management resources necessary or to consider the minority shares' economic significance (E&Y 2003/1, pp. 58, pp. 73).

According to Moelleney, the head of HR in Swissair, no real consideration was made regarding management resources. This is a hugely important concern in terms of integrating a newly acquired company because, as Moelleney said:

»The stronger they are and the better the cultural fit, the less I have to do. The Swissair board not only neglected this question but were completely uninterested in the HR concerns about acquisitions. When I spoke at meetings, board members began to make phone calls, or to walk out.« (Matthias Moelleney, during interview)

Regarding a coherent overview of the SAirGroup including indicators of costs, profitability, staff and so on, the relevant database, the MIS (Swissair's Management –Information System), was not accessible in a consistent and easily comparable format. From December 1999 forward, capital, profit and revenue were the only numbers supplied and so the system did not contain all of the pertinent information. Despite this, if one was willing to face up to the truth, the pending catastrophe of finances was clearly visible (E&Y 2003/1, p. 59, p. 76).

The relevant dangers of the project had been pointed out to the directors at various meetings about strategy. Furthermore, on a number of occasions, the board had asked the TMT to delineate the funding of acquisitions, the structure of management, and the resources necessary in terms of management. In spite of this, at subsequent meetings, the board did not monitor the implementation of the strategy. The declared circumstances, in terms of finances, were deteriorating, particularly from the second half of 1999 forwards and, a few months later, there was a financial gap of over CHF 3 billion. This was the result of the strategy's implementation which involved uncertain management resources and overdue reorganisation (E&Y 2003/1, p. 60, p. 80).

Cessation of the Strategy

McKinsey & Company's introduction on 17 August 2000, to the first phase of the Shield Scheme was the first occasion on which the board responded to the worsening circumstances. The company's financial condition was assessed, revealing a pending catastrophe, and instant measures were outlined in order to rescue the firm. More investment was halted and it was requested that opportunities to release cash were found. However, the Dual and Hunter Strategies were retained.

Bruggisser suggested a potential merge with Alitalia Airlines at the next meeting in December of the same year. Interestingly, the decision to go ahead with the scheme was taken despite insufficient attendance at the meeting to take this step. The action was totally incongruous with the previous meeting's decisions and appeared to ignore the general circumstances of the company. The Roland Berger's consulting experts were conferred with at the meeting on 22 November on the subject of possible withdrawal strategies. Once more, in contradiction to this, Bruggisser proposed the Alitalia Airlines merger again.

At last, the board confessed, but not explicitly, that the Hunter Strategy was unsuccessful in December of the same year by stating that a fourth alliance could not be created due to limited resources. The board conceded that changes to the strategy were necessary (NZZ 2001/1). As a result, Bruggisser was forced to resign the following January (E&Y 2003/1, p. 61, p. 90).

It is very interesting to note that Bruggisser said to Moelleney a few months after he was dismissed that »*he was still of the opinion that his strategy was correct, and that he should have been allowed to continue*« (Matthias Moelleney, during interview). His mistake, as he saw it, was that he had not made sufficient provision in terms of HR:

»What he underestimated, he admitted, was the management resources you need for integration, quantitatively and qualitatively – many people, that means, first, you must increase management! The Swissair Group grossly underrated that. Sabena might have been possible, but then came AOM, Air Littoral, LTU and so on, and eventually no good human resources remained.« (Moelleney, during interview)

The Relationship Between the CEO and Board

All of these acquisitions were condoned by the board of directors However, they did not use risk management professionals to assess or control the scheme. Furthermore, they often did not have complete due diligences or accurate information. This was symptomatic and a good example of this is the purchase of stakes in the Polish firm LOT. Despite the fact that the board was presented with no resources about the opportunities or risks of acquiring the firm, and the due diligence report was as then unfinished, the directors approved the purchase unconditionally. LOT's capital was suggested to be CHF 170 million shy of that given in the presentation according to the analysis in the paper report regarding finances. Furthermore, the report revealed partially incorrect and exaggerated valuation estimates had been made. This was also the case for the South African firm, SAA.

Despite the fact that it was not validated by the due diligence report on the finances, Bruggisser informed the board that there had by then been a fruitful reversal of South African Airlines' finances. In contrast, operations were still experiencing losses, according to the report. That Bruggisser was aware of this and had deliberately given the board false facts was subsequently confirmed.

Not only did they frequently lack accurate risk assessments, but often ignored them when they were available. For example, despite the fact that acquiring Air One was deemed by the board committee to be too risky, six months on they endorsed the purchase of Air Europe and the VolaireGroup so that Air One could be taken over. The committee was convinced that the required reorganisation of Air One's structure could be ably realised by Air Europe. Air One, however, was not bought.

They also did not have a vision in terms of the personnel or financial resources necessary. Unnecessarily high sums were paid for the acquisitions and spending plans were exceeded. The purchase of stakes in a French firm, Air Littoral is an apt example of this. Elevating Nice to a key air traffic centre was seriously risky, as was the financial commitment considering it was such a small earning carrier, and the analysis reported as much.

Every potential efficiency gain was already wrapped up in the top figure of FRF 200 million and further to this, in order to enable the carrier to function, another FRF 200 million was necessary in liquidity. Despite this, Bruggisser reported that merely FRF 120 million was necessary to enable the carrier to function, and that Nice was going to be an air traffic centre in the European South. Because of this, nearly CHF 300 million was an excessive price and not a valid figure according to E&Y. The real sums spent on Air Littoral were, in fact, more than had been approved according to an internal review in 2001 (E&Y 2003/2, p. 216).

Swissair ceased operations in the beginning of October 2001 as a consequence of this spending. According to one anonymous interviewee:

»The Swissair board could have asked during the Hunter Strategy, ›What is this? Stop!‹ The board should have said ›stop‹, purely as an observer. Of course Swissair can't afford to keep 49 percent of a subsidiary which goes bankrupt.« (A2, during interview)

The board's role in the strategy, and the power relations in place between the CEO and the board are not clear cut matters. One anonymous interviewee claimed the board were merely incompetent »*observers*«, who did not understand the financial implications of the strategy:

»An airline is always capital-hungry, like a hotel. To understand this, you don't need to be an expert on airplanes. You don't need to understand anything about flying or be able to fly a plane. However you must know how the financing is carried out. Also, every board must be familiar with its political environment, with international business, and know how international mechanisms function, etc.« (A2, during interview)

Another anonymous interviewee saw the board's relationship with the CEO in a completely different light and at least one significant reason for the strategy's failure as beyond the board's and Bruggisser's ability to predict:

»Yes, of course, the board has carried out its role! It was 100 percent behind the Hunter Strategy. The board even looked into the strategy; the board was informed, in great detail even. Anyhow, the Hunter Strategy assumed that the winner takes all, as in, we have to have a sound strategy within Europe. And if we implement Hunter at the right time, then it'll work. And why has this failed? One reason is 2001. Without 2001, perhaps it wouldn't have been such a disaster.« (A3, during interview)

But they were »observers« and Bruggisser was the primary force behind the Hunter Strategy. Despite the fact that a few acquisitions such as LTU were by now experiencing serious difficulties in terms of finances, the Hunter Strategy was followed when Honegger became president. Apparently, the board had faith in Bruggisser and he approved of the scheme.

The acquisitions' difficulties, in terms of finance, were starting to show more clearly as a result of the strong USD and the growing cost of kerosene. At the start of the summer in 2000, the board started querying whether the firm had the financial capability to realise this scheme. In order to ascertain the real finances of the Group, the McKinsey consultants were brought in again.

In October 2000, the board revealed that the Group were obliged for as much as CHF 3 billion and blamed the project as the source of the problems, deeming this evidence of the strategy's failure and of the necessity for instant reconsideration. The temporary decommissioning, if not the complete abandonment of the scheme, was agreed on at the meeting of the board at the end of 2000.

Bruggisser was charged with sorting out the difficult areas. The board understood that the Hunter Strategy had failed, but because Bruggisser was such a big figure in the firm, they resolved to keep to the middle ground. Further to this, he was well-liked by the Swiss and was perhaps the only individual who had a degree of understanding of all of the alliances (Luechinger 2001, pp. 230).

Board's Monitoring and Decision-making Processes

The board could not carry out their task completely, as revealed by E&Y, because the papers supplied did not conform to normal protocol as per the Group's book on regulations, and these formed the basis of the decisions they needed to make. Frequently, the directors did not get the papers in time to be sufficiently ready for the meetings. In several instances, like that of Air Liberté and Lufttransport Unternehmen (LTU), decisions were taken but the due diligence was not referred to at all. At other times, the acquisition agreements were not affected by the outcomes of the due diligence.

One anonymous interviewee claimed that this was not significant and not a basis on which one should judge the competence of a board:

»One must be very careful when making such black and white judgements because whether the board goes along with it, may or may not be a good thing. Acquisitions are much more difficult situations than many believe, and they depend on many parameters and the result can't simply be reduced to whether or not the board studied the documents and if so, how.« (A3, during interview)

One wonders on what criteria the interviewee would judge a board's competence. While review of pertinent documents should perhaps not constitute the only evidence on which to base judgement, it certainly seems a very significant place to start.

Furthermore, lacking the advantage of plans for investment because of the predominantly inefficient financial committee, the board was left on its own to make decisions on presentations. Planning in terms of strategy was not possible without an overarching directional concept for the company. In not involving itself in the finer points of acquisition funding, the board seemed to be neglecting its duties. A catastrophe resulted, therefore, from the firm's diminished resources due to the excessive employment of leveraged purchases reliant on loans made against current equity capital.

In terms of the enormously precarious acquisitions that the Group made, it is unclear if the board comprehended or was fully aware of the dangers of them and the financially complex structure which underpinned them (E&Y 2003/2, p. 8, p. 272). Frequently, exaggerated estimations of value as well as overly enthusiastic projections of profits to come were portrayed in complicated schemes representing estimations of the value of airlines and various other acquired companies. Inflated prices reflected the presumed synergies; however, in reality, projected financial benefits were normally passed on, through the high sums spent on the acquired firm, to the vendor. Because lots of the acquired firms needed extra capital injection, a careful acquisition policy would have cautiously weighed up the potential profits (E&Y 2003/2, p. 9, p. 144).

The Last Stand

By the time the board realised that the Hunter Strategy had failed, entering into an alliance appeared to be the only viable alternative, however, it would be a difficult one. While in the past Swissair would have been a very appealing partner, now they had lost much of their appeal to big alliances. In early 2001, Bruggisser was dismissed as chief executive because Honegger realised that with him in power, pushing in a new strategic direction was impossible (Luechinger 2001, pp. 257).

Over the next couple of months, no suggestions in terms of direction or strategy were made by the board. Presumably this was because the board could not arrive at a decent new strategy and Honegger had his hands full with juggling both positions of chief executive and president. Thus, becoming a member of an alliance appeared to be the only option available. Nevertheless, they had to implement many changes in order to do so: the finances needed serious attention, the majority of their partnerships were worthless, and the fleet needed downsizing,

Furthermore, the company had to relinquish the idea that it was an international leader in air travel. A hasty fresh start was vital in the circumstances, especially when the extent of the troubles was revealing itself daily. Rather than doing this, and despite the fact that its members had been on governing boards for years, the board appeared frozen or perhaps they just did not understand enough about the firm and the conditions in which it operated. By the end, apart from Mario Corti, everyone had resigned (NZZ 2001/2).

Corti came into power after a couple of months of no important changes. Corti declared the year's outcomes, in terms of finances, in April 2000 along with the initial strategic concerns he had for the company. In terms of economics, in order to balance out issues related to changing business cycles, the board settled on carrying on with the two-pronged strategy comprising airlines and connected firms. Simultaneously, the firm's structure would be pared down and, as much as was feasible, sending money out to several partner firms would decreased or cease altogether.

Thus, it would appear the board who was left at that stage, along with Corti, had really become aware of what was going on. Since the banks made CHF 1 billion available in a credit line, these strategic choices were made with the presumption that the Group had the necessary cash. Thus, the structure of finances, rather than cash availability, appeared to be the concern and so work centred on that. But, liquidity was diminishing along with the slowing of the economy. Their efforts to save the Group eventually came to nothing with the events of 9/11, a disaster which had a huge global impact, not least on the air travel industry.

In the following months, the consultants E&Y decided that there was a real possibility that the Group would be in excessive debt and this necessitated the intervention of a court. Furthermore, there were losses of about CHF 500 million as a result of swap transactions within the company's shares, which had been communicated incorrectly to the judge. A sudden increase in the firm's need for cash resulted in the declaration on 1 October 2001, that the firm was entering receivership. On 2 October 2001, as a result of this, the firm ceased operations. The consultants found, nevertheless, that at this point in time, Swissair had sufficient cash to keep operating.

Right up to the final moment, rather than taking control of the situation by making the required changes and preparing for possible problems, the top management and board depended on consultants, banks and the government to sort out their reversal of fortune. The board, however, did not have the required efficacy despite carrying out the essential official duties of efficient corporate governance.

4.5.5 Conclusion on Swissair's Strategy in Acquisitions

When the company ceased operations in October 2001, Lambert, a lawyer in a major law firm, thought that the board's role in this was not a matter to be judged by the law because diligence was too difficult to prove in an entrepreneurial decision:

»The Hunter Strategy, in hindsight, was bad. But I don't think that a judge should decide in hindsight whether the strategy was diligently prepared or not. The law suit investigates: how did the company arrive in this place, how much information did the board have, how many hours did they expend, how many times did they meet, how much paper was there, which risks were presented? If these can be proved sufficient, that they all knew what there was to know, then they made an entrepreneurial decision.« (Claude Lambert, during interview)

However, the criminal trial started in Buelach, Switzerland, in January 2007.

SAirGroup's whole board were facing charges of »mismanagement«, »false statements«, and »forgery of documents«. The key players accused included Corti, Bruggisser, Schorderet, Fouse, Honegger and Spoerry. Several of them declared to the court that they were not guilty (IHT 2007). In June 2007 the Buelach court discharged them all with regard to the original charges relating to the downfall of Swissair (BBC 2007).

Whatever the legal aspects, clearly at a board-management level, malfunctions were evident. While the E&Y report deemed the Hunter Strategy neither correct nor incorrect, it does voice serious doubts about the realisation of it and particularly its financial requirements. It is clear, however, that the problems were more endemic.

Bruggisser, the CEO, had too much responsibility, the consequence of which was that the board did not have enough influence because there was no effective communication with the management.

Only when the signals of disaster became apparent, did the compliant ethos of the board reveal itself through a lack of plans and ability to reverse the situation. As Wenger, a McKinley consultant, pointed out during interview:

The Swissair board had delegated a lot to the management. Accordingly, the board no longer had a clear understanding of how the business ran. And that's why every member of the board ended up with a liability lawsuit on their hands. (Felix Wenger, during interview)

The Group's board possessed a broad array of experience, skills and abilities, but as a team they were incapable of harnessing them, to the extent that not one of them, even if they had understood that there was a serious problem, could relate it to the whole team, according to Macus (2002).

Each individual on the board, with the exception of the chairman, had other commitments in the world of politics and/or business. Despite this wealth of experience, no one had a background in the carrier industry and they possessed no efficient risk management. Sufficient schemes in terms of finance and liquidity did not exist and resources on financial aspects were not adequate to make informed choices. In several cases, the board did not intercede if the approved financial plans were surpassed significantly, and they effectively allowed the bypassing of EU law and the instigation of the strategy.

According to the findings of the E&Y report, the process of making decisions in the Group was typically chaotic and their consequent realisation was slapdash. Fundamentally, they lacked enough information to make the majority of these decisions. On the whole, the report makes quite strong accusations and one is left with a rather sour taste.

After this, a similarly significant matter was how the board was managed. Because up-to-the-minute, integrated management was not used, the team was not especially engaged and did not possess the required mechanisms to control and monitor to the extent that was necessary to fulfil their responsibilities.

The various characters who were influential players in the final collapse of the company were also a significant aspect. Bruggisser, for example, was one of several forceful characters who had a big influence on the course of actions.

Not only Brugisser; mistakes were being made elsewhere in the firm which speak volumes about the prevailing culture. For example, to name one of many examples as to how the company was not run by market rules, a further anonymous source claimed that »*the route Zurich-Shanghai, which was a loss-making service, and subsidised by other domestic routes, was continued by Swissair because a prominent Swiss industrialist* (who cannot be named here) *wished to arrive in Swissair planes when he went to China to conduct his business. Indeed, it is not a secret that Swissair's board was part of a Swiss business ›old boys club‹ and that prominent business people would satisfy their personal business interests through their connections to the board*« (A4, during interview).

Furthermore, the public were a major influencing factor since each person in Switzerland effectively held a stake in this Swiss emblem. Indeed, the magnitude of the influence of the shareholders or citizens has, as yet, not been elucidated as the E&Y report did not look at this wider aspect.

Looking at the broader picture, as Malik (2002) stated, the top priority of corporate governance should be the strength of the company rather than serving interest groups such as shareholders and other stakeholders. In this way, a company should focus primarily on its customers in terms of delivering better products and services, which in turn enhances the company's competitiveness and market position through healthy growth.

It appears that Swissair management failed to understand the vital importance of healthy growth. Ultimately, the management focused on a combination of other factors such as management's own interest, the fulfilment of the media and public's expectations of this national emblem as well as Swiss business and political interests. In this way, they created an expansion strategy which further compounded weaknesses, leading to decreased transparency, an exponential increase in structural complexity, the dispersion of managerial resources, and subsequently the inevitable loss of management control of the company.

5. Lessons Learned About an Optimal »Leadership Environment«

As I outlined in the opening chapter, while acquisition success factors are vital, they must be supported by the *necessary leadership environment* that enables their effective implementation.

The contrasting case studies which looked at board-management interaction during acquisition and the completely different *modus operandi* of their highest governing bodies, are now comparatively analysed using Peter Drucker's acquisition principles as a framework, in order to identify the key conditions for a successful leadership environment.

Thereafter, recommendations are given to enable and create such an environment. Various board stances are then outlined which enable boards to create an effective board-management relationship during the acquisition process. Finally, this chapter illustrates that in order to be successful the board need to be able to incorporate different stances based on different corporate situations.

5.1 Comparing Nestlé and Swissair Acquisitions Using Drucker's Framework

All six of Drucker's principles are vital to the success of a business and failure to provide for any of the elements can lead to the company's eventual collapse. The first principle, that acquisition should be based on sound business strategy, is perhaps the most important as it contains aspects of the other principles and is therefore given the most consideration below. If this is not in place, no matter how well the other requirements are fulfilled, success will ultimately elude the company. As Malik (1999, p. 252) states:

»If the logic of a merger is not right, nothing will help.« (Fredmund Malik)

5.1.1 Principle 1: For an acquisition to be successful it has to be founded on business strategy rather than financial strategy.

It is important to understand that acquisition in itself is not a strategy but the result of either a *business strategy*, which is looking to strengthen a company's position in the market, its customer base, its brand and to create synergies and so on, or a *financial strategy* in which the firm's relationship with the target company operates more like that between a venture capitalist and the acquired shares.

Timing and the Timeline in Acquisitions

Timing is a key consideration. Acquisitions need to be both brave and well timed, and not just simply a way of getting out of a difficult situation. Further to this, Carl H. Hahn, an industrialist from Germany, said: *»He who restructures first flourishes; he who restructures too late threatens or destroys jobs«.* Swissair, due to a defensive, reactive strategy (as will be discussed below), could not develop timing that pre-empted market growth.

A strong emphasis on timing, in other words, having a long view was another essential ingredient to long-term success. As Maucher pointed out:

»The question of whether to operate in the long term or short term is very important and one that has to be discussed with the board as this is about strategy.« (Helmut Maucher, during interview)

Companies need a long-term vision, and in order to fulfil it, they need a well-developed strategy. When acquisitions are involved, they need to be made for reasons of furthering this strategy rather than simply as a method of expansion or to increase profits quickly in the short term. Nestlé played the long game, with Maucher often infuriating financial analysts looking at the next three years because his *strategy was for a »century«* (Helmut Maucher, during interview).

His thinking was that predictions about the market economy are often incorrect in the long term as a result of changing competition or consumer attitude, but when a long-term business strategy is used, there is more time to get ready for integration as a whole, and costs and the price of acquiring companies are usually not as big. This was in stark contrast to Swissair's reactive policies as outlined below.

Planning or Reacting when Making an Acquisition

Making an acquisition because it is part of a business plan, as opposed to a reaction to events, is crucial. If the »century« approach is in place, the company will pre-empt and plan for eventualities such as changes in the law, in currencies and markets, in politics and so on.

As an example of this, in anticipation of European developments in 1992, and their impact on Switzerland and Nestlé's position in Europe, they moved to buy Rowntree in 1988. Nestlé took the long view, acquiring companies in high-growth markets in order to remain competitive worldwide, and to increase their position in markets they understood, such as confectionary and mineral water. When acquisitions were made, they were made with a view to these clear business goals.

Conversely, Swissair was a company which developed a strategy largely as a reaction to events in the market. When the European markets changed in 1992, industrial deregulations, new rules governing landing rights and the consequent strengthening of competitors, became a huge problem for Swissair. The company reacted with several strategies in this period designed to alleviate the problems experienced in a newly opened market. It was obvious from the beginning that Swissair would not survive on its own, so the question was whether the company wanted to become the leader or only a member of an international group.

Rather than basing acquisition on a sound strategy, the TMT of Swissair were significantly affected emotionally through a process of denial, the desire to hold on, identification and attachment and therefore they could never arrive at an objective strategy. Their efforts were typified by a continual battle between the realities of an extremely competitive market and the inherent sense of superiority of the SAirGroup as a great symbol of identity in Switzerland.

Emotional subjectivity and lack of planning resulted in acquisitions based on financial strategy. They wanted simply to retain status and become bigger by acquiring firms. A hard-line expansion scheme was instigated by the firm and realised under Bruggisser's headship. By the time he was dismissed, entering into an alliance appeared to be the only viable option. Again, they were forced to react because they were not positioned well in terms of business strategy. Following Bruggisser's departure the board did not, or could not, develop a direction or a strategy. Furthermore, because Honegger was clearly overwhelmed with fulfilling the roles of both chief executive and president, an alliance seemed to be the only way forward.

Swissair's strategy was, therefore, reactive rather than pre-emptive, defensive rather than vision-based, which created a precarious acquisition policy. When a sense of urgency guides decisions, acquisitions are made in order to stabilise, to compensate for unpredicted market changes, to shore up debts and so on and while this can lead to short-term profits (but often not even this), it does not result in creating a strong company in the long run.

Developing Strategy for Acquisitions: from the Inside Out

Basing an acquisition on a business strategy is not enough; it must be a well-developed strategy based on good information and the input and approval of all involved. As such, it should develop from the inside out, using external specialists where necessary, but not relying on them exclusively.

At Nestlé, when Maucher took over he implemented an internal restructuring in order to decentralise the firm's operations. He empowered local managers, listened to them, retrieved accurate information about what was really going on and then involved the board in the process of making strategy. Advice and information came largely from within, from those »at the coalface«, and while he took on board the financial advice of outside consultants, acquisitions were based on a business strategy built on the experience and advice of his local managers and intensive discussion with his board members. In this way too, his strategy was broadly supported and this laid the ground for success.

At Swissair, conversely, throughout the various changes in dynamics between the board and CEO, the strategy was never based on wide discussion of good information.

When Swissair tried to expand into a carrier group through the acquisition of Sabena, there was a complete lack of information and resources to make a good acquisition based on business strategy. Indeed, it could barely have been classed as based on a financial strategy either. There were no documents, instead a slide show and verbal presentation formed the basis of the board of director's decision-making process. As a result, there was a great lack of comprehension and they grossly undervalued the finances necessary to sustain Sabena. It had no strategic basis as it was carried out in the interval between the Alcazar Project and the Hunter Strategy, and it occurred because an opportunity arose. Buying long-haul planes and maintaining routes that were not helping to develop the firm was one major mistake amongst others. Throughout, Swissair had a muddled approach to Sabena and it resulted in disaster.

During Goetz's reign as chairman, individuals from within the firm criticised the fact that he did not have enough knowledge about the current problems facing the company and about the industry in general. Tellingly, his CEO, Otto Loepfe, worked covertly on schemes, presenting his ideas to the board and Goetz only after he had worked them out separately. Later, Bruggisser, not only developed strategy on his own, but effectively made decisions alone. When people work in isolation, an environment cannot develop in which acquisitions can be made based on good, sustainable business strategy.

In order to develop and frame the Hunter Strategy, for example, Bruggisser, created a small expert group consisting of a few high-level managers, consultants from outside the firm and himself. As a result of merely two meetings, and with great speed, the strategy was approved by the TMT and three days later by the board committee. The TMT based their approval on the consultants' presentation which concentrated mostly on the advantages of the scheme. And three days later, Bruggisser gave this presentation to the board's committee (there is no proof that the consultants were even there). There was a clear lack of information and involvement within the Swissair culture as information did not readily flow between parties, and this is in direct contrast to Maucher's policy of staff involvement and management commitment, particularly in making acquisitions.

Where Maucher insisted on frank, open discussion and real agreement based on pertinent information, the E&Y report found that in Swissair they lacked enough information to make the majority of decisions, there were insufficient schemes in terms of finance and liquidity and no efficient risk management. They also reported that the process of decision making was typically chaotic and the consequent realisation slapdash, and in several cases, the board did not intercede if the approved financial plans and business strategy were significantly redirected. The team was not especially engaged, as they were in Nestlé's case, and did not possess the required information or mechanisms to fulfil their role in acquisition.

Thus we can see the vastly different approaches to creating strategy in the first place at both companies. It will be revealed later that while Nestlé stuck to its business strategy when making acquisitions, Swissair did not and their strategy eventually ended up as purely financially based when dealing with acquisitions.

Strategies

The next consideration is the actual shape of the strategies developed at Nestlé and Swissair. Nestlé did not want to end up as a widely diversified corporation nor did it reach towards acquisition of Nestlé's supply chain or the expansion of products. Rather, when Nestlé made acquisitions, they were guided by their own four, self-developed business rules. Acquisitions must:

Enhance market presence: Making acquisitions which enhanced the Group's overall market presence within key nations and regions and were good prospects in the long run.

Reinforce product groups: Nestlé enhanced product groups through acquisitions and made business innovations and new business lines available to the Group.

Create product group equilibrium: this policy was created in order to diminish risk through diversification in both products and markets.

Reduce the timeframe in achieving a top market position: in several instances, as well as the need to ensure the business risk remained within controllable limits, the goal was to reduce the time needed to gain a top place in a vital segment of the market.

On the whole, Nestlé did not acquire firms where the basic elements were not strong. Those that were taken over needed to have good prospects for growth in the longer run as well as technology and marketing expertise. For example, they acquired Kit Kat, a confectionary company with an innovative marketing strategy, to enhance their existing market presence. Notably, Nestlé did make two exceptional participations (Alcan and L'Oréal) purely based on financial considerations.

Conversely, when formulating their business strategy in terms of acquisitions, Swissair did not have underlying principles, and therefore targets did not have the same specificity. Frequently, Swissair's acquisitions did not strengthen their businesses, did not supply them with more expertise or innovation, did not create new clients, offer them any more protection or less risk in business, and often even involved investing a great deal more money.

Often, synergies were not considered and the only thing Swissair had in common with the targets was the same industry. Furthermore, their acquisitions had weak commercial added value because they were based on exaggerated estimations of value as well as overly positive projections of profits to come which were portrayed in complicated schemes representing estimations of the value of airlines and various other acquired companies.

When synergies were considered, inflated prices reflected their presumed financial benefits and so, the advantages were passed on to the vendor through the high sums spent on the acquired firm. Because many of the acquired firms needed extra capital to be injected, a careful business acquisition policy would have cautiously weighed up the potential profits. Swissair's did not do this.

Strategy Was Not Followed in Acquisitions

The Hunter Strategy aimed to bypass individual bilateral talks with each EEC member on rights to land (as a result of market changes after 1992 as the EEC opened up). Through fairly small share acquisition in partners, of up to 30 percent/ CHF 300 million, the strategy aimed to form a coalition between nations with prospective growth, thus redirecting routes to Zurich, its main airport, and ensuring maximum usage of the firm's long distance planes.

The Group's business strategy appeared to be a fairly good one initially in that it was founded on how the business might evolve. It took into account the potential, significant increases in the main airports of Eastern and Southern Europe. It also considered the possibilities of gaining customers through partnerships. Furthermore, it looked at the competitive advantages and synergies that would result from partnerships, as well as the possibility of more transcontinental flights in Europe alongside Germany, France and Britain (E&Y 2003/1, p. 12).

They did not follow this strategy however. The aim of expanding their own market through partnerships with national airlines whose economies were developing was only fulfilled when the firm acquired the Polish national carrier, LOT. The firm made acquisitions in mature markets in every instance besides this.

Moreover, the company frequently bought just below 50 percent (their EU stakehold quota) rather than the 30 percent stipulated in the original strategy. However, in the case of Sabenathey even ended up buying 85 percent of the airline although it made bad financial sense because Sabena did not have a positive equity-to-debt-ratio. Another instance of this was that the firm sometimes ended up with total financial responsibility, creating an open invitation for the acquired companies to increase their debt with no direct liability.

All of these purchases were endorsed by the board of directors, who, rather than looking at the acquisition strategy, merely focused on the financial aspects. Even this was badly handled, however, as unnecessarily large figures were paid for the participations and acquisitions, spending plans were exceeded, and, by the end, the majority of their partnerships were worthless.

Financial Aspects of Acquisitions

As outlined, Swissair deviated from their acquisition strategy in favour of financial considerations. Nestlé, in contrast, is an exemplary case in following Drucker's Principles in that strategic considerations like brands or the value of distribution organisations and possible synergies were more important than the paper sums, when attempting to value a firm.

Maucher distinguished and was prepared to pay more than the book value for what he felt had real value over the long term. According to Maucher, the best acquisitions made at Nestlé were actually the most expensive. Moreover, when Maucher looked to the long term, he was not concerned by the financial analysts' fears that an acquisition had a profit limitation of three years.

In the Rowntree acquisition, for example, Nestlé paid more than CHF 6 billion, an astronomic amount at the time. But Rowntree was what Maucher called a »century« buy, and was crucial to remaining competitive in the confectionary industry. This illustrates the way Nestlé put strategy at the forefront rather than financial aspects.

Monitoring Acquisitions

Moreover, while at Nestlé, the board would monitor the development of the acquisitions as to the continued fulfilment of the business strategy through detailed and thorough interaction with those who were implementing them. In Swissair, despite the fact that the board did not have proven participation in even creating the Hunter Strategy or its acquisitions, they ought to have been monitoring its evolution. According to the E&Y report, it appeared that, previous to January 1998, several individuals on the board had not even seen any paper to do with the strategy. It is quite clear they did not have a grasp of it.

Adapting the Strategy When Making Acquisitions

Adaptability was another key issue. When an aspect of the strategy did not work, Nestlé would take immediate measures; for example, because they never succeeded in generating much growth in their beauty and health areas, Nestlé sold a few of these interests, and returned to its core food products.

In Swissair, however, despite the fact that a few acquisitions such as LTU were experiencing serious financial difficulties, the Hunter Strategy was continued. The board only started asking whether the firm had the financial capability to realise this scheme when the growing cost of kerosene and the strong USD exacerbated the problems.

When the McKinsey consultants recommended the temporary decommissioning, if not the complete abandonment of the Hunter Strategy, Bruggisser was charged with the task. The board understood that the strategy had failed, but because Bruggisser was such a big figure in the firm, they did not have the strength or sufficient understanding of the situation to abandon or adapt the strategy.

Conclusion

To summarize, a clearly outlined acquisition policy was created and installed by Nestlé; the acquired firms needed to fall inside Nestlé's own industry experience and be of significance to the Group. The organisation wanted the new companies acquired to be reciprocally improving and to promote synergies through new activities. The Group's enhanced product range or presence in certain nations was a vital part of the mergers and acquisitions. As such, Nestlé mostly chose innovative companies with expertise that the Group did not have which were small or medium in size.

In terms of processes and market, the Group limited acquisitions to areas which were connected to their current or recently acquired experience or range of products. The Group did not want to end up as a widely diversified corporation nor did it reach towards acquisition of Nestlé's supply chain or the expansion of products.

Maucher only made acquisitions within the scope of the given business strategy. The strategy was discussed in close co-operation with and approved by the board. There were no surprise acquisitions by the CEO, as any takeover was in line with the strategy. The board at Nestlé got involved once an acquisition exceeded an agreed given amount. This limit on his decision-making discretion was created because »*the competence of the CEO comes to an end once a certain acquisition size is reached*« and Maucher requested that board approval be sought whenever the acquisition exceeded CHF 500 million, and the board committee's whenever it exceeded CHF 150 million (Helmut Maucher, during interview).

At Swissair, however, the ultimate goal was to purchase companies as a defence and to protect what was considered to be the true strength of the company: a truly independent Swiss brand with quality. The cost of acquisition, one might say, was the price of a defence against the »takeover of the brand« rather than a sound investment to boost a healthy growth, strengthening the competitiveness of the company based on a pertinent strategy and accurate management corresponding to the challenges.

Thus, to conclude, in terms of the above-mentioned scale pertaining to the degree of fulfilment of the principles (not at all, partially, largely, fully), it is deemed that Nestlé fully fulfilled the first principle by only acquiring firms which served the business strategy. Contrary to this, Swissair, more often than not made reactive choices based on the outlined inadequacies of the board culture and board-management relationship, and therefore, only very partially fulfilled this principle.

5.1.2 Principle 2: A fruitful acquisition has to be based on what the acquirer brings to the acquisition.

That the acquirer brings something to the acquisition is important no matter how attractive the expected synergy may look. The acquiring firm's contribution to the target can vary; for example, it could be technology, management, or even strength in distribution. Drucker specifies that this contribution must be based on something other than pure monetary investments.

The Nestlé Group brought its strong points to all of its acquisitions, enhancing aspects such as their place in the market, product range, structure of management and experience.

As an example of this, Nestlé brought their experience to the acquisition when they chose not to merge the newly taken over and up and running companies immediately (see when they first acquired Carnation). Instead, they focused on making the businesses successful in their own right, and only introducing collaboration between the different divisions step by step.

It was only after a few years that Nestlé installed a single management structure with a homogeneous organisational structure and a holding firm, so that synergies were maximised both within the company and with clients outside, helping to cement the perception of Nestlé as a corporate brand.

In order that the maximum amount of Carnation's (and those of other acquisitions') skills and knowledge were merged with those of Nestlé, certain aspects of merging were included, despite the fact that Carnation had been taken over by Nestlé. In this way, Nestlé brought their knowledge and experience of effective merging to the acquisition.

Conversely, at Swissair, no plan (and certainly not an intelligent, incremental one like Nestlé's) was made in terms of restructuring the unhealthy airline businesses they acquired. They did not restructure the acquisition's management sufficiently, largely because they did not have an interest in or understanding of the vital nature of doing this (Moelleney, during interview).

A major obstacle for Swissair in bringing something to the acquisition was that that did not know how healthy the target companies were. As the E&Y report claimed, these transactions happened very quickly without due consideration of their financing. A coherent vision was not in place as the board's finance committee did not agree with these purchases. Without an understanding of the target company, it was thus impossible for Swissair to know where they could contribute.

Furthermore, as discussed in the first principle, Swissair's primary aim in acquisition was not to integrate or develop synergies with the target companies; rather the target was seen as an addition.

As a result, Swissair made no real effort to rationalize, unlike at Nestlé where the target company was incrementally absorbed into the brand. Swissair gave the impression to the customer that there were still different companies. The obsession with preserving the elitist Swissair brand of such high quality meant they did not want to bring that to the acquisition. Swissair invested in shares rather than in companies.

Furthermore, Swissair did not rationalise the network, for example, by harmonising routes, impressing on the target firm all the more that Swissair was more like a bank or a financier who had purchased shares rather giving the impression of an airline which would absorb them. The management was dealing with acquisitions more like a holding rather than like an industrial group.

At Nestlé, contrary to this, it was vital to understand the target company, because only then would they know what they could bring to the acquisition. As Maucher said, it was important for Nestlé to »*run businesses that we understand*« (Helmut Maucher, during interview) and so he never acquired unsuitable companies.

A clearly outlined merger and acquisition policy was created and installed by Nestlé; the organisation wanted the new companies acquired to be reciprocally improving and to promote synergies through new activities.

Even the efforts to transfer competences from Swissair to the target company were undermined by not considering the obstacles to this transfer such as those created by the socially different cultures of Belgium and France. Instead, Swissair dealt with the target company as they would a Swiss one. As an example of this, in France, their 35-hour week influences the work mentality, as does their RTT (reduction du temps de travail), which means that if you work for more than 35 hours in a week you get holidays. These are used to add onto official holidays resulting in very long bank holidays. This culture of »working to live«, along with the strong syndicates to protect their rights, resulted in an inflexibility which was difficult for Swissair to handle.

Furthermore, Bruggisser used outside consultants to reproduce his own management style and did not adapt it to, for example, the French or Belgian contexts. That Swissair's board, who were experienced in the international scene, did not warn their management with regard to such difficulties compounded the problem further.

Favouring mutual consent and discussion, the Nestlé Group did not deem hostile bids acceptable, but when necessary, as mentioned above, Maucher would go directly to the companies and by bringing his knowledge and understanding, would persuade the personnel that the merger was for the best.

By managing their finances intelligently, Nestlé were able to make further investment in the company, which brought great business benefits to the acquired company and enabled the further alleviation of the social impact of the merger.

At Swissair, however, they often choose companies whose finances were in difficulty. Thus, when investment was made, money was used to repay the target company's debt, and little remained to develop the target firm from a strategic point of view.

Nestlé always operated the policy that a readiness to benefit from each other's knowledge was vital. The Group understood that a fruitful combination of personnel's experience and knowledge was one of the major reasons for the effectiveness of their M&A. Thus, a readiness to impart knowledge was an essential aspect of Nestlé's acquisition policy in terms of developing the target.

In terms of processes and market, the Nestlé Group limited M&A to areas which were connected to their current or recently acquired experience or range of products. As such, they did not want to end up as a widely diversified corporation. In this way, they could be sure that they had knowledge, resources, technology, marketing capabilities and so on to bring to the new acquisition.

As mentioned in principle 1, the ultimate goal for Swissair was to purchase companies as a defence to protect what they considered to be the true strength of the company: its truly independent, quality Swiss brand. The acquisition was the price of a defence against the »takeover of the brand« rather than a sound means of boosting healthy growth, or strengthening the competitiveness of the company based on a pertinent strategy. Hence, coming from this fundamental mindset, Swissair did not really consider the importance of contributing to the targets.

5.1.3 Principle 3: At the core of a successful acquisition there must be a common unity, for example marketing, the market, and technology or core competencies.

The companies which Nestlé acquired were in its own industry. Maucher said this was due to the fact that they had »*never entered a venture by taking a leap of faith, we always knew what we were buying*« (Helmut Maucher, during interview). Moreover, he thought that they had avoided failures by, amongst other things, buying firms within their own sector, and only those that they understood well.

Similarly, Swissair stuck to common unities in terms of keeping within the same industry (airlines), however, these were not truly pragmatic unities. Though the industry was in line with the »unity principle« the companies were not: Swissair did not examine their potential acquisitions in enough detail to see if there were technological synergies, marketing unities and so on. As explored previously, their investment logic was simply to become bigger, and cultural differences, management differences, or marketing differences were not considered pertinent to decision making.

Though Nestlé mostly chose innovative companies with expertise that the Group did not already have, these were not the only consideration, and a common core unity was always present.

When this unity existed, the Nestlé Group could bring its strong points to its acquisitions, enhancing aspects such as their place in the market, product range, and structure of management. This was a fundamental rule of Nestlé's own making. Where this unity did not exist, the firms were not acquired by the Group.

5.1.4 Principle 4: The acquirer must have respect for the target business, product, the customers of the acquired company as well as its values.

A serious risk is present when there is variance in both the management quality and corporate cultures of the acquired and acquirer's companies. Nestlé had both situations, where the companies were at odds, like Perrier, and where they were very similar, like Carnation.

The choices made and the actions taken after acquiring a company frequently affect the outcome of how well the firm manages these risks and realises a successful acquisition.

At Nestlé, a shared venture with General Mills for breakfast cereals was embarked upon because their corporate culture was akin to their own, in order to cut down the time necessary to ensure a powerful place in the market (see principle 1). Good communication between entities was enabled by similar corporate cultures and this helped to create a foundation of trust.

At Swissair, however, apart from being in the same industry, the culture and values of the target acquisitions were not seriously considered. As an example of this, the CEO imposed his own methods on the target's management and *modus operandi* and did not ask for expertise on the particular system he was getting involved in, as observed above in the French and Belgian examples. Nothing about Bruggisser's behaviour at Swissair spoke of his respect of the target companies' business, values or, as an inevitable consequence, their products or costumers.

Where Maucher was keen to be challenged and advised by his board, Bruggisser actively avoided it by limiting the information they received. With regard to understanding and respecting international acquisitions, this appears to be particularly short-sighted as his board was made up of experts who had experience in this market. They should have been a great source of information and a guide for Bruggisser in how to respect and deal with the potentially alien values, business, products and costumers of the new acquisition. In this way, respect was not something prioritised by the driving forces in Swissair. For Nestlé, it was fundamental.

5.1.5 Principle 5: The acquirer has to be ready to provide senior
       management to the acquired business within a reasonably short
       period, maybe 12 months maximum.

It is very important that the human resources necessary are prepared before a given acquisition. If a company is acquired and there are problems within the management, it is often a complex matter and it is imperative that it is fixed quickly in order to ensure the target acquisition's survival. This is a particularly serious risk if there is variance in both the management quality and corporate cultures of the companies of the acquired and acquirer.

Restructuring becomes essential, and good timing, founded on a well outlined corporate vision is a critical aspect of handling this. It is vital that the restructuring, especially restructuring associated with acquiring a company, be done swiftly. In order to handle this situation, the acquirer sends its best people in. However, if the human resources are inadequate, this will lead to a consequent dearth of good people in the acquirer's core business.

Though Nestlé always tried to work together with the target's management, as outlined in the sixth principle, they were always well prepared and able to provide management to augment the target's personnel where necessary, and this was key according to Maucher.

Contrary to this, Swissair did not understand the nature of a management transfer (as outlined under the sixth principle); furthermore they de-motivated their target management by not providing them with visible opportunities for advancement within the company (also outlined under the sixth principle); they also grossly underestimated the resources necessary and so the quick and effective transfer of senior management within a twelve month period was never realised.

The E&Y report reiterates this. It found that Swissair failed to consider the extra funds and management resources necessary and as a result, they ran out of good human resources.

Bruggisser even said to Moelleney a few months after he was dismissed that what he had underestimated was the management capacity needed for integration, quantitatively and qualitatively. Bruggisser learned this the hard way. It may have been possible to cope with Sabena, but the successive acquisition of AOM, Air Littoral, LTU and so on made more demands on the human resources of Swissair than they could sustain and they could certainly not fulfil the fifth principle's short timeline requirements.

Moelleney reiterated this himself by pointing out that:

»Important questions that a board has to ask are ›How much of my own human resource capacity do I need to build in order to be able to integrate the new company? The stronger the target acquisition, the better the cultural fit, and the less I have to do (...)‹ But the Swissair board neglected this question. What is important in relation to this (in addition to the financial and legal due diligence) is a HR due diligence where one can study the partner firm in detail.« (Matthias Moelleney, during interview)

The problems at Swissair were further compounded by the fact that they did not take human resources seriously. That the board hugely undervalued his input was illustrated by Moelleney, the head of HR, in the way that the board walked out or made phone calls when it was his turn to speak in meetings. It is difficult to see a well-prepared strategy for providing senior management to the target company in a short period evolving from this attitude.

Furthermore, Bruggisser's policy of enforcing his own management methods on the target acquisition, as in the case of Sabena for example, and refusing to acknowledge local specificities, would have created a very slow and inefficient integration of the inadequate amount of senior management provided.

Lastly, at Swissair, the board did not monitor the strong management personalities in the subsidiaries, but limited its scope to the top management of the core company. Their attitude as »venture capitalists« meant that they considered the subsidiary management as already integrated, which is not the case, as explored under the next principle. At Nestlé, as Philippe de Weck pointed out in interview, the board would ask difficult questions on every aspect of the provision of senior management for the target acquisition: did they have the right people? Did they have the resources? And so on. A clear disparity of approach is evident once again between the two companies.

5.1.6 Principle 6: In a successful acquisition clear opportunities for advancement must be visible in both the acquired and the acquiring business.

Despite the fact that many of the measures involved in restructuring protect jobs in the long run, it is important to remember the individual's experience and the personal upheaval that M&A entail.

Alleviating the effects of a restructuring process through a successful series of social measures is obviously beneficial to the firm. Nestlé's TMT understood that this is a fundamental precondition for an effective acquisition policy in the long run.

The longevity of Nestlé's success was founded on trust, and in order to keep it, Nestlé had to supply enough assistance to its personnel, and make opportunities for advancement visible, in order that they could adjust to new systems or secure alternative employment. From the outset, this was a foundation stone of Nestlé's approach.

Along with making sure that promises were realised and, as a vital psychological element, that overall integration happened swiftly, Nestlé focused especially on equal opportunities and motivation of the acquired firm's executives. Vital functions in Nestlé were given to many executives from firms acquired by the Group.

In contrast, Swissair was not looking to highlight new opportunities available to the management of newly acquired companies. As size was the main justification for the acquisition in the first place, they were not looking for sustainable growth in which management and industrial structures were in sync with the extension of the company. Target companies were made to feel like they were bought by a venture capitalist.

According to Maucher in interview, when acquisitions or mergers are declared these days many executives of firms »*who carry out an acquisition, believe that they are the clever ones and the others are stupid*«. Indeed, in a way this could be said about Swissair. As mentioned above, they tried to impose their own *modus operandi*, irrespective of cultures and current system. Often they got rid of staff without even having sufficient replacements.

Furthermore, even the reporting tools used by TMT at Swissair took too long to establish and were, as demonstrated, hugely inadequate. The board simply did not really understand what was happening in companies such as Sabena or LTU and they did not object to this. They were not interested in the experience of the target companies' management, never mind in providing visible opportunities for advancement.

Indeed Moelleney's experience as head of HR during board meetings is a very apt demonstration of the lack of importance placed on the experience of the acquired company's personnel. Advancement never even made it onto the agenda.

In stark contrast to Swissair, Maucher, prioritised visible opportunities for advancement. For example, when Stouffer and Carnation were acquired, their heads eventually became the heads in America. He also understood the important psychological motivations associated with this and their critical role in acquisition success. He considered »*leadership, motivation, and involvement of these people*« (Helmut Maucher, during interview) instrumental in this success. Nestlé, under Maucher, avoided psychological mistakes such as imposing management on targets, creating frustration and resulting in the eventual departure of good people. Nestlé also avoided letting target management go or creating an atmosphere in which they were demotivated through being side-lined.

Even in hostile takeovers Maucher did not veer from this principle. In the case of the semi-hostile takeover of Rowntree, for instance, Maucher went to the company the next day to personally assure the employees that they would have many opportunities for advancement as part of a bigger

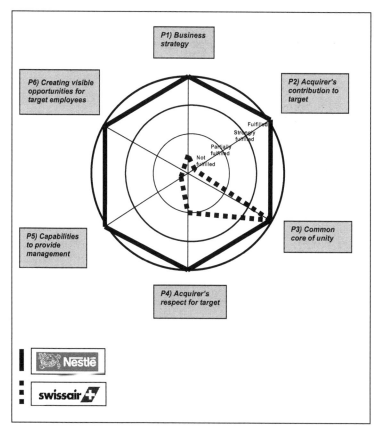

Figure 3: Fulfilment of Drucker's principles at Nestlé and Swissair

company. In this way, a framework was created in which the abilities of the acquired company's personnel were respected and recognised and gradually they were absorbed into new opportunities within the Group. Hence, intrigues and power struggles which typically follow an acquisition were prevented or at least minimised.

Once again, Nestlé made every effort to fulfil the sixth principle resulting in successful acquisitions which were integrated and mutually enriching. Swissair, however, set the visibility of opportunities for advancement as a very low priority, lost a lot of excellent personnel in the target companies as a consequence, and did not realise successful acquisitions.

5.1.7 Conclusion

Figure 3 constitutes a summary of the analysis, which reveals the polar nature of these case studies. Swissair did not fulfil any of Drucker's principles with the notable exception of principle 3, although on closer examination this was proved to have been fulfilled merely superficially. Nestlé, in contrast, had a very successful acquisition strategy, which from an external point of view was implemented with no mistakes. As demonstrated, Nestlé fulfilled all six of Drucker's principles entirely.

5.2 Creating an Environment that Enables the Acquisition Principles to be Successfully Implemented: A Comparative Analysis of the Case Study Boards

The question addressed in this chapter is: *how did the board of directors contribute to creating an environment that enabled the acquisition principles to be implemented successfully?* Having used Drucker's six principles to examine Nestlé and Swissair's acquisition success, the underlying or more fundamental conditions are now explored: the environments. The leadership environments (the company's orientation, the board-management structure, its functions, power relations and interactions) in the two case studies were clearly different because in Nestlé's case, the six principles were fulfilled and in Swissair's they were not. An examination of the Swissair and Nestlé boards' respective contributions to this environment follows below.

5.2.1 Recruitment

Swissair's board did not always recruit internally, as was consistently the case at Nestlé. In fact it was almost a doctrine to do so at Nestlé, in order that potential CEOs were tested and knew the culture and the business very well, from its strategic to its industrial specificity. More importantly, candidates are a known quality in terms of their reactions, strengths and weakness and there is no room for excellent self-marketers who give good interviews. But by recruiting outside the company, the board at Swissair were losing both the valuable specificity of insiders and the opportunity to test a potential CEO in the longer run.

Another way in which the Swissair board did not take due consideration, was that they did not adapt themselves to the change initiated by the CEO selection; for example, the internationally experienced board members did not educate Bruggisser on integration matters and cultural differences in France and Belgium. Furthermore, they did not re-engineer their procedures to bring these cultural and internal expertises to the CEO. A change of recruitment method could have instigated a change in board influence so that it could provide more input to the CEO.

5.2.2 Board's Relationship with the CEO

At Nestlé, the board's relationship with the CEO was one in which the board shared the vision of the CEO who was also chairman. The CEO gained the board's approval through rigorous discussion, questioning and communication. At Swissair, however, the board had an almost passive relationship with the CEO. As discussed below, they did not question his decisions and policies, they did not insist on access to relevant information or time to digest it, and they did not monitor the implementation of a strategy in which they had little involvement.

In contrast, at Nestlé, Maucher had a very inclusive attitude to the board despite the fact that he was the driving force in the company and it was not a requirement. He was attentive to the valuable input from the board, he actively sought advice and even insisted the board committee travel the night before a meeting in order to ensure they had studied the relevant documents. In this way, the CEO and board were pulling in the same direction at Nestlé, and the board approval and their powerful support created a constructive environment in which the six principles could be fulfilled.

5.2.3 The Board's Role in Terms of Leadership and Strategy

In terms of the board's role, at Nestlé they did not seek to have a managing role in the company but rather to support the management. They acted as guardian of the global vision of the firm by looking for acquisitions which would create real synergies with the existing firm, synergies which were enjoyed by both companies. This was reflected in the fact that the board had to be called upon to approve strategic extensions related to a specific M&A. This meant no acquisition was made without being of strategic significance. The board was therefore able to veto any acquisitions which were not justified by a business strategy and this meant that the board had the job of ensuring the business coherency of acquisitions.

The board at Nestlé functioned in a controlling, analytical and advisory capacity rather than looking for operational involvement. This gave a real strength and legitimacy to the CEO for implementing the strategy he had designed. The board at Swissair, however, appeared to a large extent to have outsourced its role to external consultants in terms of contributing to strategy. Where Nestlé used consultants as experts on ad hoc basis to add a competence that was missing on a particular project, Swissair's board went so far as to relinquish their advisory role to external consultants.

Not only was the board at Swissair the advocate of a strategy in whose creation they had had very little involvement, they did not rigorously monitor the implementation of Bruggisser's strategy or the pertinence of the wave of acquisitions to the company's goals. Significantly, they did not question the use of liquidity in terms of the real development of the targets or the investment policy. Instead, they allowed Swissair cash to be spent on paying targets' debts rather than on financing growth.

A good example of this is that the board did not stop deals in which the Group was obliged to guarantee the targets' debts, as in the case of Sabena and Airlib (previously known as Air Liberté). This became an open invitation to these companies to spend funds without having to justify the expenses. As a result, this guarantee and subsidy was permitting these companies to retain highly inefficient cost structures. The money flowing into them was not connected to an obligation to restructure or instigate a sustainable growth plan which would involve a sound investment plan. This was in direct contrast to the board at Nestlé where mutual synergies were carefully analysed including cost considerations.

Nestlé's board was also highly attentive to the sustainability of the firm and as such, regularly requested information about the state of the brands and their individual current potential. This included questions about new products, products that were being »retired«, a product's life cycle, cash flow, market share and so on (see correspondence from de Weck to Maucher in chapter 4).

Furthermore, the board at Nestlé asked rigorous questions about all areas of the company: the coherence of acquisitions with the established strategy and the industrial and commercial needs of the Group. More particularly, the board was made up of bright, independent people who were not afraid to ask difficult questions at difficult moments regarding resources (including human), targets, management and so on. In this way, they ensured the fulfilment of the acquisition principles. This is in direct contrast to the board at Swissair who were not inquisitive about the state of the company.

5.2.4 Board Preparations

Much of the above was a consequence of the availability of information (or lack thereof). At Swissair, there was a significant lack of preparation for board meetings partly because the documents were only made available at the beginning of the meeting, and partly because the information provided was not clear and comprehensive. No meaningful reflection was possible, therefore, because the CEO had, effectively, prevented it.

Despite this, the board did not react to the absence of regular information from the management and was not proactive in trying to get this input to aid their work. Getting the approval of the board was more important to the CEO than convincing or consulting them. Opacity became the unspoken rule and the board never tried to change this.

Again, a great disparity exists between the *modus operandi* of Swissair and Nestlé. At Nestlé, while Maucher provided limited information in terms of volume, it was extremely relevant (such as Maucher's thirteen pages to the board on a given acquisition). Maucher preferred to put his time into creating pertinent short documents rather than providing reams of excessive information, with a view to making the meetings more efficient. Furthermore, under Maucher's instigation, the board gathered a day before meetings for consulting the documents. This enabled board decisions to be based on the relevant facts.

5.2.5 Serving a Nation's Myth or Serving a Company

At Nestlé, the board was made up of independent members who respected their CEO but were prepared to argue with him, ask difficult questions and demand answers. They were not bound by the social significance of being part of an iconic company, by the financial benefits (they were indeed all wealthy), and nor did they relax into a state of »laisser faire«. They served the interests of Nestlé, not their own or their other companies, and critically, this enabled them to keep the ultimate goals of the company in mind when making decisions on matters like acquisitions.

At Swissair, there was an absence of clear goals in terms of satisfying or creating clients, and this not only hampered the constructive exchange between board and management, but was a result of operating within the myth of Swissair. For this reason, focus concentrated more on the brand than on the real health of the company. Whereas at Nestlé, the brand was a means to an end (to strengthen the business, competitiveness and sustainability, and eventually to satisfy clients and costumers), at Swissair, it was an end in itself. As such, the board became the defender of an image which it perceived as the company's main asset.

Swissair was not run and managed by the »rules« of how a corporation in a market place should be managed. Based on faith in the Swissair myth, the board's actions were further affected by the accepted idea that the company was as much there to serve the Swiss economy as its own development because an airline is a systemic strength for a country.

Moreover, the interest defended by the board was also the interest of the other companies they were leading for which Swissair was functionally vital. They were thus divided between Swissair, and how it could contribute to the growth of leading Swiss firms. Lastly, Swissair, as a symbol of Swiss quality, served the board members' own sense of national identity. This obsession with brand and the absence of industrial perspective partly explains the inertia of the Swissair board when facing the absence of vision in terms of strategic development.

Indeed, it is also fascinating to see the manner in which the strategy at Swissair was influenced by national sentiment in relation to strategic development. There is no doubt that the nation was adamantly against outsiders in terms of foreigners running their national flag carrier and that they considered Swissair valuable to them and this influenced the popularity of the Hunter Strategy. That the company had never been a private enterprise in this way was revealed by the partners in interview.

As discussed above, the Swissair board, in contrast to Nestlé, was not a proactive partner to its management; they were effectively letting the CEO control the strategy. Indeed, the board refrained from challenging the management because, as discussed, they felt the main interest of the company was its brand and their role was to defend it in the face of public expectations.

With the board focused on external shareholder interest, the implementation and monitoring of a sustainable business model, the primary role of a board, came a poor second. It is not a coincidence that when the press spoke about Swissair, the eras of the chairmen were more commonly referred to than the CEOs'. This is in stark contrast to Nestlé where the CEO is used in the chronological definition of an era. This is significant because it shows that the board of Swissair operated more as a PR institution than as a regulatory body of governance. In this way, they mainly functioned as a representative board; the board, with a prestigious composition, became more of an exhibited circle to promote the company than a truly active and vital institution performing their tasks.

5.2.6 Preliminary Conclusions

Thus, the Nestlé board made the system work. Their policy on recruitment for both the board itself and the CEO was effective. Furthermore their relationship with their CEO was active and their preparation for meetings consistently good. They developed strategy with their CEO which served the interests of the firm and they fulfilled their duties as a board in every aspect. In contrast, the Swissair board had a precarious recruitment policy for both their CEO and board members who had other interests in the company. They developed an ill-conceived strategy and then did not stick to it or monitor acquisitions, particularly in the area of liquidity. Ultimately, they behaved as a representative board, a symbolic rather than functioning body, largely as a result of their persistent attachment to the myth of Swissair.

5.2.7 Summary

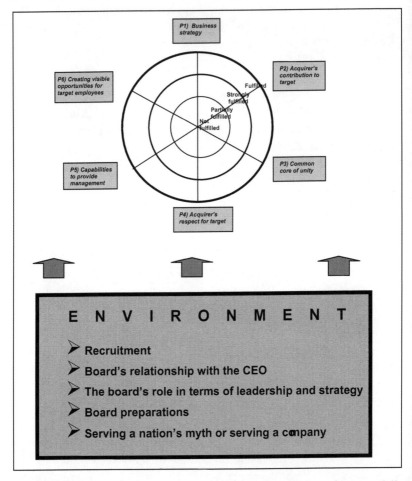

Figure 4: Environment that enables the acquisition principles to be successfully implemented

6. Twelve Best Practice Recommendations for Boards

6.1 Creation of a »Leadership Environment« Which Enables the Acquisitions Principles to be Fulfilled

Building on the above discussions and insights, several best practice recommendations can be deduced with regard to the duties of boards in the context of corporate acquisitions. Through adhering to these best practice recommendations, an environment (in terms of the company's orientation, the board-management structure, its functions, power relations and interactions) can be created in which the acquisition success principles can be fulfilled. By respecting the best practices as outlined below, boards can establish processes that are more effective at delivering acquisition outcomes compared to many current corporate models.

6.1.1 A Clear Definition of Whose Interest the Board Is Serving as well as Board Involvement in Fixing the Basic Strategy

The board needs to know what and whose interests it is serving. The interest of the company and ultimately its clients should always be the priority and not stakeholders, as was the case in Swissair, where the TMT attempted to serve a variety of stakeholder interests simultaneously. The board and management must agree this interest and also the exact nature of the needs of the companies' customers. This creates a transparent environment in which the company's orientation is clearly understood, a foundation on which good business conditions can flourish.

Only when this is in place can a clearly outlined strategy be created. This should be co-developed by the management and board and periodically revised. Based on this strategy, goals can then be derived which are to be achieved through acquisition. As discussed previously, extensive studies have shown that more than half of takeovers fail. Takeovers are connected with high risks. These risks can be reduced only by the existence of a clear strategy.

As illustrated in the empirical section, if the underlying strategy is not good and hence the subsequent reasoning behind the merger or acquisition is not in place, then nothing will help. The development of this strategy, therefore, becomes the central challenge of the M&A process and is the first responsibility of the board of directors. It is vital that an acquisition respects the fixed underlying strategy which was approved by the board (even if the board was not actively involved in the original elaboration of the strategy, but approved it subsequently). In this way, from the outset, there is agreement as to whose interests are being served and how they can be served through a strategy. This creates an environment in which the TMT are pulling in the same direction, using the same language and this creates a framework for healthy, constructive discussion on the future development of the company.

More specifically, with acquisitions, by contributing to the development of the strategy, the board of directors can exert great influence on M&A activities. In addition, the board's perspective on the firm's strategy constitutes a valuable input for the top management as their distance from the day-to-day business allows board members to critically challenge the elaborated concepts with a measure of objectivity. This again enables the board to contribute to the M&A process through enhancing an environment in which the management and board bring various levels of perspective (micro and macro respectively) on the firm's strategy and its implementation.

6.1.2 Added Value Approach

A major element which impacts the environment, as the Nestlé case study revealed, is what Maucher coined as the added value approach. This is realised when the TMT is focused on how it can add value to the firm rather than simply exercising formal authority. This approach should permeate all levels and activities of the company and can only be realised if each employee is highly involved and working towards the same goal. With this, special assignments and project work are more likely to push through the traditional boundaries of authority. At board level, this task-based *modus operandi* can be achieved through installing a board committee, as witnessed in the Nestlé case study.

Generally, in terms of realising the added value approach, companies should be costumer and result oriented rather than system oriented. Though systems are required, the TMT should ensure that they are not an end in themselves. For this reason, when customer confidence and retaining customer loyalty is the primary focus, boards must make sure that a culture of long-term thinking permeates all management activities.

More specifically, in terms of realising this added value approach on an organisational level, it is important to ensure an appropriate management structure which is flat and flexible. An organisation which is as decentralised as possible in order to be adaptable creates a constructive environment with fewer levels of management.

Finally, in order to create added value on a management level, it is vital that the board ensures clearly defined goals, levels of responsibility and accountability. TMTs must make sure that capability is maximised through a flexible, task based approach. This is key. In this way, Maucher attempted to figure out at what point he added value or provided gainful input in the debate, and otherwise handed over matters, even when technically the final choice ought to be made by him. Thus, the TMT works less through job titles and the powers associated with them and more by intentionally generating added value for the firm.

The board must ensure that this added value approach is deeply embedded in the corporate culture and constantly maintained. This creates the right environment for success on every level: the company's orientation based on customers; the board-management structure involving, for instance, a board committee; and optimalised interactions through a task-based ethos.

6.1.3 Global Outlook, Operating with Local Specificity

»The board has to apply the Matrioschka System: Acquisitions should be conducted top-down, bottom-up and laterally, and all these approaches should be linked to each other. This is the ›Glocal Approach‹.« (Martin Hilb, during interview)

Hilb's »Glocal Approach« is a combination of thinking globally and acting locally through the relevant local employees who are familiar with the geographical, cultural, political and business specificities.

Further to involving local employees, board diversity is once again crucial as boards of directors who are active on an international scale can help management understand the specificities of the socio-economic systems and bring valuable local expertise. In this way, the board gains contributions from directors with understanding of the acquired management and learn of possible caveats linked, for example, to socio-cultural factors. In so doing, the board facilitates an environment in which expertise flows easily between bodies, enriching interaction and ultimately creating an enhanced awareness of socio-cultural matters, enabling the acquisition success factors to be fulfilled.

6.1.4 Composition in Terms of Special Expertise

Specialist skills are vital and a member of the board who possesses applicable skills to a deal should contribute them. Moreover, the board should only employ external expertise if this is deemed necessary. Special expertise should be found in a well-diversified board with directors of various and complementary experience. Board composition is decisive in getting a range of special expertise. Furthermore, the special expertise inside the board should be given priority and be able to contradict external experts, especially if the board members' expertise is specific to the field in question.

Ideally, the members should have experience associated with the company and its markets. This experience gives the director the opportunity to identify developments in the environment and to estimate their effects on the company. This is concluded despite Maucher's view that for a board member a critical mind enjoys priority over knowledge of the company and industry. At Nestlé, this worked because Maucher was a brilliant leader, but it seems more likely that a board who understands the industry is more likely to ask the right questions and be capable of meaningful contribution. In this way, an environment is created in which there is enhanced interaction and critical examination of proposals. With a deeper level of discussion, there is an increased likelihood that the relevant success factors are identified, considered and reviewed.

In conclusion, each member of a board of directors should have expertise in a relevant area and must make sure the board is aware of this competence. In this way, they are capable of critically and competently evaluating the problems concerning specific areas and the board becomes a pool of capabilities the CEO can mobilize in a particular situation. As the case studies revealed, however, should this requirement not be fulfilled, the board can still be successful. In this situation, the board should mainly focus on the diligent fulfilment of the acquisition process and making sure that they receive the key information and relevant experts' opinions in order to make decisions. By doing so, an environment is created where the board is optimising its function as monitor thereby making decisions on M&A necessarily more fruitful.

6.1.5 An Active Board Committee for Strategy

When analysing a potential acquisition, along with the latest projected figures and relevant information, an active board committee is vital. As illustrated in the Nestlé case, a small, well-informed committee with expertise and good communication with the CEO can efficiently contribute, monitor and serve a transaction. This is because they are more active, for example by meeting more frequently, and gain a more in-depth knowledge of the matter under consideration. In this way, the committee has the potential to be a highly effective means of keeping the board connected to the daily operations of the company.

They also work alongside the CEO, act on behalf of the board on less major decisions, and, along with the CEO, equip the board to make more major decisions. As a delegation of the board, the committee introduces another level of decision making, acting as a middle ground. Thus, the board committee maximises the board's function through generating more levels of decision making. This fosters an environment which enables the effective implementation of acquisitions and optimizes interaction and the board-management structure.

6.1.6 Identification of Appropriate Acquisition Targets & Mobilising Expert Knowledge to Review Targets

Board expertise not only helps members to ask the right questions at meetings, but their special contacts can also be harnessed in the search for targets for takeover by using them to identify suitable companies. Many boards of directors have extensive networks of relationships, which can be of use in many respects. *Firstly*, these relationships enable the initial identification of appropriate targets. *Secondly*, the board members know many companies due to personal contacts in top management positions and thus can provide additional inside knowledge to augment (perhaps even contradict) the due diligences that are mostly confined to economic and technical data. Building on these connections, the board of directors can also establish first contact with the selected targets in order to facilitate access and to foster a friendly environment during the execution of the takeover. In this way too, potential hostilities are minimised and the later integration process is facilitated.

Furthermore, following the identification of a takeover target, more detailed assessments are often necessary. Although specialist knowledge is required, board members who possess the necessary expertise are often asked to conduct the assessment. This is often the case with lawyers, for example, who can support the management with legal advice. Another example is technicians, who can provide valuable assistance in the evaluation of production sites or products. In this phase, only select members are asked for advice; only in rare circumstances do the whole board get involved. Thus, when selecting target acquisitions, both connections and special expertise create an environment in which resources are maximised and interactions enhanced, in which there is a greater chance of identifying the best target acquisition which, in turn, lays the ground for successful implementation of the acquisition principles.

6.1.7 Consideration of the Management Proposal after Target Selection

An extremely important duty of the board is the critical examination of the management proposal after the selection of the takeover target. The board of directors has to consider the proposal with a sole view to the interests of the company. *Firstly*, it is necessary to clarify that the acquisition or merger is in line with the basic strategy of the company and that its goals can be achieved through the intended acquisition. *Secondly*, it is vital for the board to ascertain if there are sufficient human resources available in case the target management leave the firm. *Lastly*, the board must ascertain if the planned mutual synergies can be realised and if the expected profits are realistic. It is worth noting, however, that an objective evaluation is often very difficult to conduct because the board of directors is influenced by the opinion of the management. The board is then no longer capable of performing their supervisory function. Indeed, Malik (2002) points out the need to for the board to make provision against the management's influence:

»Is it sufficient if the executive provides information in an open and generous way? I don't think so. The supervisory body should, actually must, be able to get his own information from independent sources.«

Malik goes on to explain that it is a delicate situation, in which the board must find the balance between getting the right information but without doing too much so as not to undermine the CEO and his authority (Malik 2002).

Thus, the board must examine the management proposal in terms of strategy, resources, synergies and profits. Moreover, they must find an objective method of analysis in order to limit the influence of the board and retain their supervisory role. In this way, a critical and objective environment is fostered in terms of the examination of the management proposal and, by ascertaining an objective understanding of the acquired firm, the board enables the six principles to be realised.

6.1.8 Integration of the Acquired Company

Another way in which the board can help to create a healthy environment is in the assistance they can lend the CEO when trying to integrate the acquired company. Such measures mainly consist of building the confidence of a company after a takeover and include taking into account the acquired firm's internal and external culture, providing equal opportunities to all personnel, implementing the Group's *modus operandi* with moderation as well as working alongside the acquired firm's management.

A board can not only share its knowledge of work culture variance in different countries and within companies but can select a management who integrates corporate culture in its practice. In addition, it is crucial that they continue to question the CEO on the integration process and to monitor the results. In this way, the board nurtures an environment in which integration can occur smoothly, thus increasing the possibility of the acquisition's success through the application of the six principles.

6.1.9 Full Disclosure

An important contribution from the board in creating an environment which fosters good interactions is in the promotion of transparency. Full disclosure is vital in that boards should make every effort to ensure that the CEO and his team give the board complete information in terms of the target acquisition. It is critical, however, that the information is condensed down to its most crucial parts, so that the board can use the information provided to make a sound decision in an efficient way. The case studies revealed that long, complex and detailed decision documents are counter-productive and do not enable useful discussion. At Nestlé, most complex deals were presented on 13 pages or less: this allowed for full and transparent disclosure, but was still sufficiently condensed for the board to make an informed decision in a reasonable time.

Furthermore, all information on real and possible clashes of interest should be revealed. The board must also ensure that the CEO and his team give accurate information together with projected figures. Therefore, the appointment of a CEO who trusts the board as much as the board trusts him is critical to an environment in which there is free circulation of information and, therefore, healthy interaction. It remains crucial, however, that the board also seeks information from independent sources in order to preserve its uncompromised supervisory function. As discussed, this becomes a delicate balance in terms of getting accurate information without undermining the CEO's authority. If handled well, an open environment develops in which the principles can be realised and acquisitions can thrive.

6.1.10 Clarity about the Board's Role & a Proactive Relationship Between Management and Board

It is vital that the role of the board of directors is understood by the CEO and his team. It is the board's task to supervise and monitor the CEO. Moreover, from the outset of the deal, the board ought to clarify with the CEO which decisions will be made by the CEO and his team and which will be made by the board (beyond the board's original agreement to do the deal). In addition, the two bodies should agree on the type and frequency of board meetings, as well as the information the board want to review before, during and between these sessions.

Moreover, it is important for both bodies to understand that monitoring does not mean infantilisation. Monitoring is a questioning process which protects the future of the company and improves the CEO's reflection. The questions asked by the board should be designed to improve effectiveness and the CEO's capacity to implement strategies. In turn, the CEO should not treat the board as an alternative source of strategic creation but rather consult with the board to strengthen the legitimacy of his strategy.

As explored when looking at board-management models, extreme power imbalances between the two bodies are not effective. Ideally, the board is neither a second management (as it was in Swissair in its first phase) nor the management a second board (Swissair in its second phase). Rather, the board should instil a co-operative relationship with the management in which there is mutual trust. This is also fostered if the board shows its intention to remain a board and not to become a concurrent management. The board is then a proactive, independent entity which asks questions and necessitates active persuasion by the CEO.

As such, a board should not behave as a tribunal. It is not a competitor of the CEO, it is an institution protecting the interests of the company and ensuring M&A are aligned to the company's strategy. The CEO remains in the driving seat but the board monitors the CEO, if he is running the company effectively along the lines previously agreed and if the M&A are in line with this strategy.

In this way, the board does not, by itself, make an acquisition successful but it is vital in creating the environment for the acquisition principles to flourish by filtering the acquisition through the validated strategy and supporting the management's reflection process.

6.1.11 Accepting That the CEO Remains the Key Figure

»If the company is run well, the board is superfluous; if it's run badly, the board is helpless.« (Helmut Maucher, during interview)

Though many boards assume that they are the most important body in a company because the law grants them ultimate responsibility, this clearly does not reflect the reality. As discussed, the CEO works full-time, compared to the board's relatively infrequent meetings, is the closest to the business and has the greatest understanding of it. It is therefore crucial to understand and accept that the CEO is the key figure in a company.

While the board must accept that they are not in the driving seat, this does not mean that they do not have impact. The CEO is responsible for developing the basic strategy and the subsequent M&A and must persuade the board of the validity of his plans based on full disclosure of his thoughts and actions. The board adds value by bringing a degree of objectivity to this, a macro perspective. The board critically examines, questions and approves the CEO's actions. In this sense, they have the final power.

Finally, the board must also safe-guard the limits of the CEO's power and avoid the case where »*absolute power corrupts absolutely*«.

In this way, if the board is aware of the above key insights in terms of the powerful role of the CEO, the importance of full disclosure and the corrupting influence of absolute power it is not superfluous. The board takes effective action once a company is being mismanaged, as it can recognise this in early stages before a disaster occurs. Referring to the opening quote, when a board is armed with these insights it is no longer »*helpless*« because it can identify inadequacies early on and take action. The board's most critical point of impact, therefore, is in recruiting the right CEO.

In conclusion, recognising the CEO as the key figure in the company enables an environment in which there is clarity about respective roles and duties. In recognising the CEO's power the board-management relationship is described accurately and the board is hyper-aware of the critical importance of full disclosure in their interactions. The board and the CEO should mutually agree on high level boundaries of the CEO's power such as needing board approval for acquisitions costing more than a given amount or occurring outside the approved strategy. This ensures that major decisions are made on a sound basis and an environment exists in which constructive processes are available.

6.1.12 Succession Plan for the Key Figure of CEO

With the insight that the CEO is the key figure in a company, the topic of succession planning becomes crucial for maintaining a healthy environment and a company's long-term success. It is vital that the board is aware of this duty, particularly if the CEO has a strong personality who typically avoids having other strong personalities around him. This results in a weak pool of people for the next CEO. In contrast, Maucher, though strong, surrounded himself with strong people. As countless examples bear witness, successorship becomes a source of serious problems on boards where it is not prioritised and contingencies are not made.

If a successorship plan is not in place, a destructive vacuum occurs in which rivalries arise that are damaging to an environment with healthy interactions. Thus, in a weak position, the board are forced to find a solution quickly and usually choose under a great deal of pressure. Often, external, uninitiated people who are not familiar with the company's culture are brought in to plug this gap.

If a solid succession plan is in place, however, there is certainty and transparency. Most importantly, a well-thought-out plan allows for a »stress test« of future leaders: they are well-known to the board giving a sense of continuity; they have been with the company for a long a time and have an engrained added value approach; and their true values in times of crises have been observed. As a result, internal jostling for position does not create factions, a smooth changeover results and business can continue uninterrupted.

The environment is thereby enriched through a sense of stability and continuity, avoiding vacuums, crises, and rushed, ineffectual appointments.

6.1.13 Summary:

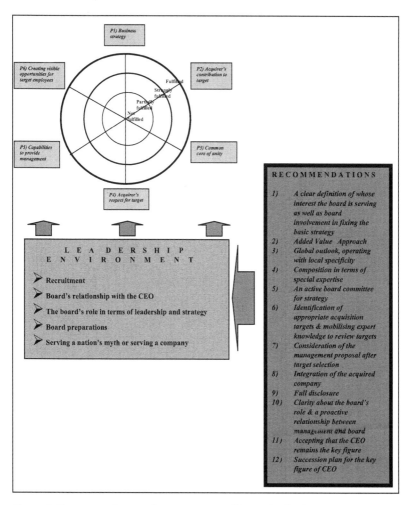

Figur 5: Recommendations for creating an effective leadership environment

6.2 A Dynamic Board-Management Relationship

Besides the relationship between the board and CEO, its equilibrium and the quality of exchange, another important aspect revealed through doing the empirical field research, was that the board's stance was of great importance. Indeed, these aspects were discovered to be largely interdependent and as such, mutually defining: the relationship between the board and the CEO dictated the board stance and vice versa.

6.2.1 Theoretically Reasonable Board Stances

The regulator of board duties has produced several different interpretations as to how a board should be organised. Accordingly, several quite different board models are conceivable, each of them implying different activities and characteristics of the board of directors. These can co-exist and overlap. Building on Puempin (1990), a range of theoretically reasonable board stances are outlined below, as well as their significance in an M&A context:

The Representative Board

Particularly in public companies with strong management, the board of directors has a very limited influence on the business operations. The board functions more like a supervisory board as designed by German law. To underpin the prestige of a company, these boards are often key representatives of important political groups, e.g., members of parliaments, association representatives or former top-ranking officials.

The representative board of directors only meets a few times a year. During the meetings, several standard agenda items are discussed, such as the company results or budgets. The board's most important duty is that of exercising its control function. Participation in the creation of company policy or other entrepreneurial activities is hardly expected in this model.

Due to its significant distance from the day-to-day business of the company the representative board of directors is only marginally involved in M&A. Acquisitions are entirely controlled by the management, who only inform the board of directors on a regular basis. In this stance, the board of directors only contributes through their extensive business connections. As explored above, Swissair's second incarnation under Bruggisser saw the board lapse into a representative stance, as a body overly concerned with its PR and brand mythology. At Nestlé, however, a representative stance was used only in the sense that the law demanded that a certain portion of the board be Swiss. In this sense, there were always members who had a representative role. Nevertheless, it never became the governing stance.

The Knowledge Board

In this model, the board of directors is normally presided over by a person who is also an active member of the executive board. In addition, the board is supplemented with several experts who function as specialists in specific areas: lawyers are the most common, who take charge of legal issues; in technically oriented companies, there are specialists from corresponding areas of technology; and finally, auditors serve as specialists in areas such as financial accounting and auditing on the boards of directors.

It is crucial in this model that board focus is not on the overall firm strategy and business development, which are sporadically discussed at best, but rather the operational management. The chief executive is the driving force in defining the strategy and will do this at his sole discretion.

The board members therefore contribute with their specific knowledge on matters: the lawyer will be asked for legal advice, the natural scientist for advice on technical issues, the auditor for questions about accounting and so on. Matters necessitating referral are principally solved on an individual basis and, in general, they are not discussed at the board's official meetings. Furthermore, the knowledge board assumes, to a certain degree, a control function, but this is not its primary role.

The knowledge board model is used in many medium-sized firms, but also in bigger companies. It usually consists of a larger number of board members and the board meetings are conducted in a very formal way.

In this model, the M&A activities are conducted mainly by the management; however, they specifically seek the advice and input of the board which has expertise in different areas. The overall contribution of the board to M&A activities is therefore limited to selective expert assignments. At Nestlé, for example, the board moved into a knowledgeable stance when Maucher called for specific legal advice from Bueckli or financial advice from de Weck (Helmut Maucher, during interview).

The Entrepreneurial Board of Directors

An entrepreneurial board is one which includes entrepreneurial members. Building on Maucher (2007), entrepreneurs, as opposed to managers, are individuals whose objective is to innovate and create rather than supervise and create routines. Where the manager predicts and plans for the short term, the entrepreneur uses her imagination and vision for the future and looks to the long term. A manager makes decisions based on rational evaluation of pros and cons where an entrepreneur counts on his intuition and creative interpretation of the information in difficult situations; in this sense he has the personality of a leader. A manager sees his duties within a company whereas an entrepreneur sees mainly entrepreneurial opportunities outside the company. The manager administrates and optimises the company using his technical competence, but the entrepreneur adds to this by being strategically oriented and a corporate developer; as such, he is inspirational. The manager hedges risks whereas the entrepreneur takes risks and has courage. The manager works with analysis, goals and measures whilst the entrepreneur works with simple concepts and basic ideas that he follows uncompromisingly.

In terms of stance, the entrepreneurial board model not only benefits from specialists' contributions and fulfils its control function, but the top management expects an active participation in shaping the company. In the legal sense, the board of directors should deal with the essential issues that affect the existence of the company. In this capacity, the design of company policy and even important business activities belong to the board's responsibilities. The entrepreneurial board typically consists of personalities who are elected due to their experience as entrepreneurs and managers. This kind of board of directors has recently gained popularity and is often found in successful companies.

Entrepreneurial boards are a great resource in M&A activities because they think and are motivated like owners and always assume accountability for their actions. A good example of this is the way in which Nestlé's board acted through their board committee in order to be close to the business; in this manner, the board could face the business challenges alongside management. In this sense, they were not only a formal body but a proactive and involved one. Because entrepreneurial boards have a proven track record of creating and developing businesses they can be of critical help to the management during the acquisition process. This ranges from targeting using their extensive networks to contributing with their intuition on how to proceed on a specific deal and its integration, as ultimately each deal is unique. Hence, the entrepreneurial board stance is best for coping with complex issues related to M&A and forms the basis for successful acquisitions.

The Active Board of Directors

This model comes closest to that demarcated by the law. Board members fulfil tasks related to both operational management and business operations simultaneously. Thus, the board of directors and management are, to a large extent, identical. Typical examples of this model can be found in many small and medium-sized family enterprises, where the entrepreneur is president as well as delegate of the board of directors.

In this stance, the board has an active role during acquisitions by taking on management duties and thereby becoming the driving force in M&A activities. In this model, the board is capable of leading the M&A process and handling the corresponding risks. Swissair in its first phase, when the CEO was very much subservient to the board, is a good example of this. In fact, it resulted in the CEO implementing strategy he did not agree with. Conversely, the board at Nestlé only moved into this stance if a member had specific connections at a target company and could therefore operate as a point of contact. This was only ever used in a limited way, however, because Maucher was a strong and involved CEO who would take charge before long.

Other Types of Boards of Directors

For the sake of completeness, it should also be mentioned that in particular situations other types of board models are, in principle, possible. In Switzerland, for instance, according to Art. 711 Abs. 2 OR, the majority of the board of directors must consist of Swiss citizens. One would expect that some Swiss companies with foreign-dominated capital are likely to elect board members solely on the basis of their Swiss citizenship, despite the fact that an international board of directors may be more appropriate.

6.2.2 Creating an Effective Board-Management Relationship for Smart Acquisitions

It was revealed in the theory section that a board is capable of adopting many different stances based on what the situation or specific acquisition required. Nestlé is a good example of this, as outlined below, becoming an active, knowledgeable, entrepreneurial and representative board as the situation needed. On the most part, however, they took up an entrepreneurial stance, the ideal, but remained adaptable. At Swissair, in contrast, they only ever assumed two kinds of stances, representative and active, and neither position proved successful in the longer term.

6.2.3 Conclusion

Thus, Swissair's board took up two stances during the periods covered in the case study. At first, they were an active board, as the driving force behind acquisitions such as Sabena. With the rise to power of Bruggisser, they relinquished their powers and subsided into a representative board, as discussed previously. In contrast to this, Nestlé was, on the whole, an entrepreneurial board; however, they were capable of changing their stance when particular acquisitions called for it.

It can also be deduced that the *entrepreneurial stance is the ideal model;* the board operates through a few entrepreneurial board members in a committee which is closer to the business and this enables them to constructively contribute to business problems while still respecting the Hilb's board doctrine of »*keeping your nose in but your hands out*«. The relationship between the management and CEO in this stance is excellent in that both parties get the most out of it; the CEO gains access to valuable internal resources and added value leadership and the board benefits from a much stronger understanding of what is happening on the ground.

Today's business world is undergoing faster and more significant changes than previously experienced, based on an increasingly globalised world. In order to cope with these changes, it is becoming ever more important that the management is supported by entrepreneurial personalities. Because they think in the long term and have great qualities of commitment, these personalities have the necessary tools to continuously evaluate the organisation, its challenges, staff, and structure. With a board like this in place, it is the management's prerogative to use the board as an expert resource and sounding board. Therefore it can be concluded that having an entrepreneurial board of directors is the best precondition to meeting the challenges of M&A and developing effective solutions.

Though an entrepreneurial stance is ideal, the *ability to move between stances in different situations is the key.* For example, if an acquisition is an exceptional situation or an acquisition is outside the agreed strategy, then increased input from the board is necessary and it becomes appropriate that they move towards being a more active board. Another example would be if the CEO were in the process of deciding whether to enter into a new geographical market or a different product group; then the ability of the board as an internal resource to move into a knowledge stance would be of great advantage to the CEO. The board would be capable of providing a unique viewpoint on the matter from within the company to which external consultants are not privy, such as internal strengths and weaknesses or cultural aspects. Hence every case is different and a board has to be capable of adopting stances which reflect the needs of a given situation.

To conclude, an adaptable and proactive entrepreneurial board is the ideal model. Nestlé serves as an excellent example of this, operating usually as an entrepreneurial board (with representative aspects), as a knowledgeable board when expertise was needed on a project and as an active board when a particular connection existed between a board member and the target firm.

6.3 Summary

Literature, law, and corporate governance define the board as the main governing body in an organisation. As the majority of acquisitions still fail, the starting point of this analysis was, therefore, to look at the role of the board in M&A. The reality, however, proved very different. It was revealed by the case studies that the CEO is, *de facto*, the most powerful person in the firm despite, *de jure*, the board being the key body with ultimate responsibility.

The board delegates its responsibility, which *is proof of the discrepancy between action and responsibility, reality and law.* This structural discrepancy radically disempowers the board, a merely *pro forma* body, as it cannot have an impact if the CEO does not proactively involve it.

An extraordinary CEO who always puts the interests of the company and its customers first can negotiate this. However, as there are a limited number of Mauchers in the world, this cannot become a template to be generalised.

Nevertheless, by respecting the twelve best practice recommendations for boards and the adaptable board stances as outlined above, the resultant board-management relationship can create a constructive environment in which the principles can be fulfilled, resulting in successful acquisitions in the current framework.

The in-depth analysis of board-management relationships in M&A revealed the fundamental structural inadequacies in the current corporate governance and legal system and are discussed in the conclusion below. These structural inadequacies are becoming increasingly critical, particularly because of the changing nature of acquisition forms in a business world of increasing complexity. *Radical solutions are needed.*

7. Conclusion

In this last chapter an exploration is made of the movement of M&A towards new and diverse forms of co-operations which are different to traditional acquisitions. The current, very visible limits of the corporate governance system are revealed through the research and most strikingly the discrepancy between legal requirement and practical reality. Clearly, *new forms of corporate governance need to be urgently prioritised*. Thus, an attempt is made to offer innovative structural solutions to cope with these complex challenges.

7.1 Outlook: The Changing Nature of M&A

7.1.1 The Rapid Increase in M&A: the Actual Significance

Up to the present, there have been many sudden increases in M&A and new waves will occur again when the economic crisis has been alleviated. The sudden increase in M&A a hundred years ago at the turn of the 20th century was probably the largest and most significant recorded in the United States. It established the vast bulk of large corporations that lead the American economy right up to the 1960s and 70s. These included, amongst others, the GEs, the United States Steel Corporations, the GMs, Alexander Graham Bell's AT&T, associated companies under Rockefeller, etc. This was also the case in Europe, for example, with Siemens.

Since then, several other sudden increases in mergers have happened in Europe and the US. In the final years of the 1920s, many small firms merged establishing the bigger utility-chemical firms such as Steel-Union, the Interessen-Gemeinschaft Farbenlndustrie AG, or its corresponding British firm, Imperial Chemical Industries. Furthermore, during this time several larger British and German banks merged. These developments resulted in a consolidation of the number of corporations in the market.

7.1.2 The Changing Nature of Acquisitions

Mergers in the past were used as an »offensive tactic« with a view to enhancing prosperity and profit. Most of the mergers nowadays, however, are designed as a defence to decrease the rate of deterioration. In a vulnerable or contracting sector, the best method of stopping or reducing this is to reduce expenditure. Spreading the outlays to larger companies which the firm acquires is the simplest method in the short term and this is currently the reason behind numerous large mergers. It is unknown if this has the required effect in the longer run.

Nowadays, despite continuous mergers there is no more consolidation. Rather, with each large acquisition, very often a number of parts are sold to small or medium-sized firms. Thus, there is a deliberate division of large firms creating a number of autonomous firms. Indeed, more than 50 percent of the acquisitions in 2009 were divestitures (Insite 2010). Furthermore, it looks probable that this will increase. Recent examples include Rio Tinto acquiring Alcan in 2007 and thereafter implementing a broad disposal programme, or the Vodafone-Mannesmann deal in 2000. Subsequently, Vodafone disposed of several of its businesses. Very recently, Solvay sold its pharmaceuticals business to Abbott.

The origins of this trend may be in the beginning of the 1980s, when Welch took up the position of chief executive at General Electrics and declared that the firm would dispose of any of its parts that were not capable of securing first or second positions globally. While Welch's decision was a completely original idea at the time, over the last 20 years or so it has become a trend, transforming global business.

Usually, a firm becomes healthier and more concentrated as a result of demerging, and often gets smaller. The awareness that diversity is becoming progressively more difficult in the global markets is a possible explanation for the current acquisition and disposal trend. In order to prosper, firms have to concentrate on their strong points within their core businesses. Also, the tendency to source large sections of the production procedure outside the firm is another reason for many demergers. In this case, a firm makes a deal with another one to carry out certain aspects of the process such as taking care of the firm's IT, HR and training, accounting, caretaking and upkeep, and the buying of supplies apart from a small number of essentials. The extent of this in today's business is not entirely clear, but suffice to say, almost all large firms (and indeed smaller ones) contract out huge sections of their business that, until recently, were internal affairs.

To conclude, though demergers and mergers are always at the centre of media attention, they are not likely to be the most significant aspect of the future structure of corporations and even economies. Rather, new and diverse organisation of firms' structures and strategies will constitute the key means of business evolvement.

7.1.3 Moving from Acquisition Towards a New Form of Cooperation

In the future it is likely that acquisition will lose ground with regard to fostering a corporation's prosperity. Largely unmarked by the media, and generally unperceived, the real changes seem to be happening *as alliances: joint ventures; cooperative deals* in relation to marketing-research technology etc.; the case where a large firm purchases a minority share in a smaller firm; and frequently, »handshake deals« which *do not involve many law-based or formal contracts* to support them. In this manner, for example, the pharma sector has, on the whole, edged into fresh technologies like those surrounding the science of genes (Fritz Gerber, during interview). Previously, buying a firm in the new sector of the industry, or less frequently, making its own advancement in this sector would have been a large and reputable firm's way of manoeuvring into the sector.

Currently, the usual way of doing this is through a deal that prevents the large firm from gaining power over the operation, like the many deals between American universities' science departments with global pharma firms.

Nevertheless, whether law- or finance-based, numerous alliances resist conventional classification. By way of an example, how might one define the nature of the alliance in 1995 between Sony and Intel (or Ericsson) which, it is said, was agreed with no formal, written deal? For Sony, the conception of a personal computer and the production of its key parts in terms of electronics will be carried out by Intel. As a direct competitor with the main buyers of Intel's products, Sony will put together these parts and sell the personal computer in America. No monetary investment, either way, exists between the firms and both cover their own overheads. Sony benefits from the design expertise at Intel and they, in turn, benefit from the fact that their latest microchip has a certain and exclusive buyer. Undoubtedly, this does not figure as either a typical joint venture or deal based on expertise.

Recent examples of such joint ventures include Rio Tinto and BHP Billiton, a joint venture to combine their Western Australian iron ore assets and share infrastructure. Another example is the joint venture between Société Générale and Crédit Agricole to cooperate with regard to their asset management business. Furthermore the joint venture between BP and TNK to jointly proceed with oil and gas exploration in Russia is worth mentioning.

It is interesting to note that the Securities and Exchange Commission does not need notifying of these associations. No sums are printed. On the whole, they require little investment and therefore can go unmentioned in an audit.

By law, the paper work involved is very similar to that drawn up for service vendors or suppliers. But in terms of the economy, it involves operating alongside each other as partners and is supposed to be a long-term effort. Far greater than the number of M&A, the number of these alliances is undoubtedly very big.

Financial concerns are not the major consideration behind these new kinds of relationships. Finding the necessary funds to acquire companies or make their own advancements in the area would not be hard for large, reputable firms. Rather, *a new way of thinking is behind the shift.*

Previously, it was generally accepted that all businesses could operate under the same type of management structure. Harold Geneen, who established a huge firm based on acquiring firms in the 1960s and 70s, was a particularly strong advocate of this theory. In incredibly diverse sectors, he made over 300 acquisitions. Moreover, he was sure that by transplanting uniform systems and fund monitoring, they could be effectively managed and prosperity would follow. Indeed, as long as he was at the helm, the company's ITT was celebrated in the stock market. Once he left in the late 70s, however, the firm began to deteriorate.

Nowadays, we are starting to recognise that even though there are general ground-rules of management, their implementation and relevance may need to be adjusted for variations in markets, IT, internal cultures, and, primarily, the particular business theory used.

7.1.4 Are Current Corporate Governance Structures and Management Methods Capable of Dealing with These Changes?

These new forms of relationships between organisations alter our conception of what constitutes leadership, because *no one is in control* when relationships are constituted of partners and allies through co-existence. With no leader, there is no one to answer to; in the same way, no one serves. A person who is *leader of one project may be the follower in the next*. For example on a business operation which requires cultural specificities, an expert with this cultural and legal background would be most apt to run this project. The same person may only operate on the peripheries of the next deal, as only some of his skill and experiences are relevant.

Although these new relationships involve co-operation, the companies still operate autonomously in order to achieve individual targets and fulfil individual duties. As a result, previous methods of managing M&A relationships, founded on ownership and control, will not function under these new kinds of co-operations. In contrast, these relationships are founded on *equality, rather than ownership, trust rather than control*, and they *last only as long as both parties benefit*.

These joint ventures and alliances, as opposed to the old model of M&A, will, therefore, *require new management and governance structures* in order to realise their potential.

7.2 Current Corporate Governance and Future Challenges

The understanding that the board was the most important body in a firm was the jumping-off point for this book. This is supported in literature, by law, and in the opinions of many board members who were interviewed during the empirical research. For this reason, the role of the board was placed as the primary consideration in the research question in order to understand why acquisitions fail or succeed.

Based on the analysis of M&A governance and empirical investigation of leading CEOs' and chairmen's opinions about the reality of managing acquisitions, the following was revealed:

Firstly, the board's influence is currently *over-estimated*: the board is widely considered to be the most important body in the firm, the »brain« and the driving force. In reality, as leading international CEOs such as Maucher, Gerber and de Weck revealed through in-depth discussion, it is the CEO who is the real mover within the company. In this sense, the board is merely a *pro forma body*, its overarching influence »wishful thinking« on the part of the large majority of board members and those dealing with and writing about boards. But it is, in fact, ludicrous to think that the board could run a company if they only meet, at best, once a month. The maxim that »knowledge is power« holds true here. The CEO is in daily contact with every aspect of the business, he is »on the ground«, most knowledgeable about the industry and his staff and he chooses what is reported back of this. If he is a good CEO, then the best attempt at a partial reckoning is made at these meetings, if not, as in Bruggisser's case, the CEO has the power to deliberately withhold or influence the clear understanding of the board. Thus, in reality, as per the Nestlé case study, *Maucher made the system work* by actually giving the board influence in order that they could meaningfully contribute, but ultimately, *he still ran the company*.

Secondly, reflecting on the reality of the CEO-board relationship, the fundamental reason for the fact that the CEO is so powerful (besides the fact that he is closest to the business and most knowledgeable about his industry and his staff etc.) is *structural in nature*. Currently, the relationships between a company's bodies are ultimately governed by legal and corporate governance requirements as these decide ultimate responsibility. These laws and requirements were created because of previous corporate failures and so *lawyers* and *financial experts* were brought in to draft laws and recommendations to avoid future mistakes. They formulated this, as is the nature of laws, in terms of »*what is forbidden or to be avoided to prevent failure*«. Thus, in order to appease the law's need for accountability and, critically, to decide *who goes to jail* when failures occur, organs were created and boundaries strictly delineated in Art. 716 (for the Swiss situation) which outlines the responsibility of the board.

The law saw that the board was the *highest body* in a company (though this has been revealed to be only superficial) due to its role as advisor and monitor and therefore assigned the board *ultimate responsibility*. At the same time, it allowed the board to *delegate many of its responsibilities*, including its role as strategy maker. In practice, the board does delegate this to the CEO because it is not *de facto* involved with the actual running of the company. This can only be interpreted that *the board is not in a position to exercise its given duties*. There is clearly a discrepancy. The board should not be responsible for something if they are not actually doing it. Moreover, because the board is delegating, it means that they are doing this because they cannot fulfil the tasks themselves. So why are these tasks given to the board in the first place? It appears that the current legal context is clearly not appropriate.

In this way, the problems with the relationship between the management and board are further compounded by law and corporate governance. As discussed, if the CEO does not actively involve the board, it is difficult for the board to fulfil their role. The argument that the board could fire the CEO if they thought he was insufficient or that the board were being given limited information is not valid because, in reality, the board would not necessarily know that they were not »in the loop« until it was too late. Furthermore, when the CEO is also the chairman, this means that effectively the CEO is electing his own board. The CEO can therefore influence board composition; a strong personality might bring in weaker people or people who do not understand the industry and will not ask pertinent questions. Again, *the system requires that the CEO is an incorruptible entity and capable of almost inhuman impartiality.*

As noted in the interviews with the leading CEOs, the CEO becomes much more powerful due to the his proximity to the business, the fact that the board only meets once a month, the board delegates many of its duties, and the legal structure invites the CEO to take risks without incurring responsibility and so on. Absolute power begins to focus on one individual and the *danger »of absolute power corrupting absolutely«* becomes real. The system only works when a strong personality, such as Maucher, takes the helm.

Maucher was brilliant and *made a flawed system work.* Critically, he was not egocentric and even had the personality and foresight to make arrangements for a successor, realising that big personalities leave huge power vacuums on their departure. One could compare it to a *dictatorship* in that if the right man is in power, it is the best form of governance and the most efficient, but if the wrong man holds absolute power then disaster on a large scale is inevitable (»l'État, c'est moi«). Democracy, therefore, becomes the lesser evil and the safeguard from great disaster.

Thus, several interesting conclusions have arisen. Building on the title of this book and the original premise that the board is the major mover in a firm, it is now clear that, counter to intuition, the *CEO is the key force* in the company and in acquisitions. This is in line with Maucher's belief that the main cause of failure is a CEO corrupted by vanity:

»You can't have people in this position who are too vain, get carried away, or become obsessed with power. They need to exercise their power because that is part of their job. But if these people become irrational then they are in the wrong place.« (Helmut Maucher, during interview)

As a result, Maucher believed that for an acquisition to be a success, the board's crucial role was not increased involvement but simply hiring the right CEO.

While the empirical research in this book has borne out this idea, it is too limited and there are other vital elements to acknowledge in acquisition success. The *relationship between the board and management,* as discussed, is vital and it also *dictates the board's stance* (and vice versa). Furthermore, the board, *ideally an entrepreneurial* one, need to request effective information packaged in a concise and useful way (as was the case in Maucher's reign). This enables efficient meetings in which pertinent questions can be raised and informed decisions made. Transparency should be a key note. Lastly, because of the key nature of the board-management relationship in successful acquisitions, the board need to *recruit their CEO internally*. It is vital that the board know their CEO well, have tested them under a variety of situations and are therefore aware of their strengths or weaknesses.

Based on the insights above, several factors are necessary to a successful acquisition: *a cooperative CEO*; *a board that is entrepreneurial* and, importantly, is *a dynamic body which can adopt various stances*; and *a good relationship between both bodies*. This, in turn, creates an environment in which the six acquisition principles can be fulfilled.

In this way, the current corporate governance system can be effectively negotiated, even compensated, using the best practice recommendations. Nevertheless, this does *not* address the root problem, which is that *the legal structure and current corporate governance do not reflect the reality of business* and *nor is it likely that they will be able to cope with the business world of the near future*. As explored previously, we are entering into a very different business world due to the changing business practices and global business interaction. Broadly speaking, acquisition is being replaced by cooperation, partnerships, joint ventures and new, lateral structures in terms of hierarchy and so on. If the current corporate governance cannot even cope with the current business world, it will become an increasingly serious problem in the future.

Corporate structure would also benefit by *moving from a hierarchical system to one based on competence*. This would alleviate the problems associated with a hierarchy in which people work for recognition, for example, to please the CEO, as opposed to being results-orientated in order to climb the hierarchical ladder.

Moreover, corporate structures which are *not so much body-based but function-based* would further engender a dynamic mode of operation as opposed to a static one. This is not to suggest that bodies ought to be dismissed as organisational structures but that more fluidity should exist within them where emphasis shifts towards function. In this way, the system would be better able to cope with the joint-venture global business world currently emerging where, for example, research bodies from different companies often combine efforts while their TMTs continue as separate entities.

This would also play a part at an individual level: jobs would be based *not so much on the job title but on the skill set* of the individual. In this way, individuals have the potential to operate in many capacities on different projects, thereby maximising their usefulness. A more dynamic system is thereby created, which is more independent of bodies and job titles.

Maucher was moving in this direction when he restructured the TMT under his policy of »*as much hierarchy as necessary but as little as possible*« (Helmut Maucher, during interview). He also insisted that the TMT worked less through job titles and the powers associated with them and more by intentionally generating added value for the firm. On a broader scale, Maucher recognised:

»(…) more principles and fewer detailed regulations are needed because, fundamentally, these regulations do not fit every company« (Helmut Maucher, during interview).

By institutionalising what Maucher started with his »value added« policy, the role of the board would be to enable the »*best fit for the deal*« or »*staffing for strength*« in terms of positioning the most suitable people for a specific project who bring the required knowledge, experience and skill base. Each project has its own unique needs and staff requirements and therefore people are allocated on a value added basis, changing their role and position from one acquisition project to another. Furthermore, it would be advantageous if the board could work as a dynamic force by itself, independent of the CEO, rather than dependent on a Maucher to be an initiating force.

Just as Nestlé had dynamic board stances, dynamic roles could create the same strengths. In this way, the CEO could be a changeable entity or have lots of different roles, and operate more like a project manager. Thus, concentration of power in the hands of one person would be avoided as would the inherent risk involved.

Perhaps, like Malik (2008) suggested, the CEO's role could be divided amongst five people because, again, there are a limited number of Mauchers in the world. A democratic institution would develop in this case.

Whatever shape future solutions might take, the fundamental problem today is that the current corporate governance system is riddled with problems which result from inadequate reaction to context. The key point is that corporate governance should provide answers to the questions of *how the environment should be structured so that the board can lead effectively* and *what makes good leadership and management?* These are much more relevant and

important questions than the question corporate governance is currently attempting to answer, that of how failures can be avoided in the future.

Discussion Partners

Despite the fact that two in-depth case studies were the subject of this book, the research sources were set to be much greater than this in order to grasp a more wide-ranging view of the business world with regard to the topic under discussion. In alphabetical order, the following people were interviewed between 2006 and 2010:

Nestlé board members: **Dr. h.c. Fritz Gerber,** Nestlé (former board member), Roche (former CEO and chairman), Zurich Financial (former CEO and chairman); **Mr. Bruno Kalbermatten,** Nestlé (former board member), Bobst (former CEO and chairman); **Dr. h.c. Helmut Maucher,** Nestlé (honory chairman, former CEO and chairman); **Mr. Philippe de Weck,** Nestlé (former board member), UBS (former chairman)

Board members of other Swiss multinationals: **A1 – made anonymous on request,** CEO and chairman of several companies, Close to several board members of Swissair; **A2 – made anonymous on request,** Board member of several companies, Close to several board members of Swissair; **A3 – made anonymous on request,** Board member of several companies, Close to several board members of Swissair; **Prof. Dr. Roman Boutellier,** SIG (former CEO) & member of management in several Swiss companies, Professor for innovation and technology ETH; **Prof. Dr. Rolf Dubs,** Schindler (former board member); **Prof. Dr. Karl Hofstetter,** Schindler (board member); **Dr. Arthur Loepfe,** Arbonia (board member); **Dr. h.c. Thomas Schmidheiny,** Holcim (main shareholder, board member, former CEO and chairman), Swissair (board member); **Prof. Dr. h.c. Wolfgang Schuerer,** Holcim (board member); **Prof. Dr. Rolf Watter,** Syngenta (board member), Zurich Financial (board member), Nobel Biocare (board member)

Swissair board members and experts: **A4 – made anonymous on request,** Swissair (board member); **Mr. Matthias Moelleney,** Swissair (former member of the executive board, Head of HR); **Mr. Sepp Moser,** Swissair (aviation expert, aviation journalist); **Mr. Walter Vollenweider,** Swissair (former member of the executive board)

Experts (academics, consultants, lawyers and investment bankers): **Ms. Bettina Bornmann,** KPMG (Partner, Head of Corporate Finance); **Mr. Peter Dammisch,** BCG (Partner); **Dr. Alberto Francheschetti,** Bain & Company (Partner); **Mr. Joost Geginat,** Roland Berger (Partner); **Prof. Dr. Martin Hilb,** University of St. Gallen (Professor of Business Administration), Institute for Leadership & Human Resource Management, University of St. Gallen (Managing Director); **Mr. Philipp Hofstetter,** PWC (Head of Corporate Finance); **Dr. Stephan Hostettler,** Hostettler & Partner AG (Managing Partner); **Dr. Marc Macus,** University of St. Gallen (Senior Research Associate); **Prof. Dr. Fredmund Malik,** University of St. Gallen (Titular Professor), Malik Management Zentrum, St. Gallen (chairman); **Prof. Dr. Guenter Mueller-Stewens,** University of St. Gallen (Professor of Management), Institute for Leadership & Human Resource Management, University of St. Gallen (Managing Director); **Dr. Claude Lambert,** Homburger (Managing Partner, Head of M&A); **PD Dr. Urs Schenker,** Baker McKenzie (Managing Partner); **Mr. Dieter Turovsky,** Morgan Stanley (Managing Director, Head of M&A); **Dr. Felix Wenger,** McKinsey (Partner)

Bibliography

Achleitner, A. K. & Fingerle, C. H. (2003) ›Unternehmenswertsteigerung durch management buyout‹, *EF Working Paper Series*, no. 01–03, München.

Ahuja, G. & Katila, R. (2001) ›Technological Acquisitions and the Innovation Performance of Acquiring Firms: A Longitudinal Study‹, *Strategic Management Journal*, vol. 22, pp. 197–220.

Allen, J., Lummer, S., McConnell, J. & Reed, D. (1995) ›Can Takeover Losses explain Spin-off Gains?‹, *Journal of Financial and Quantitative Analysis*, vol. 30, pp. 465–485.

Amabile, T., Patterson, C., Mueller, J., Wojcik, T., Odomirok, P., Marsh, M. & Kramer, S. (2001) ›Academic-practitioner Collaboration in Management Research: A case of Cross-profession Collaboration‹, *Academy of Management Journal*, vol. 44, no. 2, pp. 418–431.

Anderson, C. R. & Paine, F. T. (1978) ›PIMS: A Re-examination‹, *Academy of Management Review*, vol. 3, no. 3, pp. 602–612.

Andrews, K. R. (1980) ›Directors' Responsibility for Corporate Strategy‹, *Harvard Business Review*, vol. 58, pp. 30–42.

Ansoff, H.I. (1981) *Corporate Strategy: An Analytic Approach to Business Policy for Growth and Expansion*, Harmondsworth.

Anson, M. (2004) ›Trends in Private Equity in 2004‹, *The Journal of Wealth Management*, vol. 7, no. 3, pp. 84–92.

Ashby, W. R. (1970) *An Introduction to Cybernetics* (5th edition), London.

Auerbach, A. J. & Reishus, D. (1988) ›The Impact of Taxation on Mergers and Acquisitions‹, in Auerbach, A. (ed.) *Mergers and Acquisitions*, Chicago.

Bathala, C.T. & Rao, R.P. (1995) ›The Determinants of Board Composition: An Agency Theory Perspective', *Managerial and Decision Economics*, vol. 16, no. 1, pp. 59–69.

Barkema, H.G., Bell, J.H.J. & Pennings, J.M. (1996) ›Foreign Entry, Cultural Barriers and Learning‹, *Strategic Management Journal*, vol. 17, pp. 151–166.

Baumol, W. (1967) *Business Behavior, Value and Growth*, New York.

BBC News, ›All Swissair Defendants Cleared‹, (2007), BBC1, 7th September 2007.

Beatty, R. & Zajac, E. (1994) ›Managerial Incentives, Monitoring and Risk Bearing: A Study of Executive Compensation, Ownership, and Board Structure in Initial Public Offerings‹, *Administrative Science Quarterly*, vol. 39, pp. 313–335.

Becht, M., Bolton, P. & Roell, A. (2002) *Corporate Governance and Control.* ECGI – Finance Working Paper No. 02/2002, European Corporate Governance Institute.

Bender, C. & Vater, H. (2004) Audit Committees – Motor einer ganzheitlichen Unternehmensüberwachung auch in Deutschland? In H. Vater, C. Bender, C. and K. Hildebrand (Eds.), *Corporate Governance Herausforderungen an die Management-Kultur* (pp. 75–88). Bern: Haupt.

Bettis. R.A. *Performance differences in related and unrelated diversified firms.* Strategic Management Journal, 2, 1981, pp.379–393.

Biland, S. & Zahn, P.A. (1998) *Verwaltungsrat als Gestaltungsrat.* Zürich.

Biland, T. A. (1989) *Die Rolle des Verwaltungsrats im Prozess der strategischen Unternehmung: Führung, Planung, Implementation und Kontrolle von Strategien in der Spitzenorganisation Schweizer Aktiengesellschaften.* Unpublished Dissertation, University of St. Gallen, St. Gallen.

Bilimoria, D. & Piderit, S. K. (1994) Board Committee Membership: Effects of Sex-Based Bias. *Academy of Management Journal, 37*(6), 1453- 1477.

Bleicher, K. (1989) *Unternehmungsverfassung und Spitzenorganisation: Führung und Überwachung von Aktiengesellschaften im internationalen Vergleich.* Wiesbaden.

Böckli, P. (1994) *Die unentziehbaren Kernkompetenzen des Verwaltungsrates.* Zürich.

Böckli, P. (2004) *Schweizer Aktienrecht mit Fusionsgesetz, internationalen Rechnungslegungsgrundsatzen IFRS, Börsengesellschaftsrecht, Konzernrecht und Corporate Governance* (3rd ed.). Zürich.

Boudreaux, G. (2005) Peter Drucker's continuing relevance for electric cooperatives. *Management Quarterly, 46*(4), 18–32.

Boulton, W. R. (1978) The Evolving Board: A Look at the Board's Changing Roles and Information Needs. *Academy of Management Review, 3*(4), 827–837.

Buchmann, P. (1976) *Organisation der Verwaltungsrate in 20 der grössten Aktiengesellschaften in der Schweiz.* Bern.

Berger, P. & Ofek, E. (1995) Diversification's Effect on Firm Value. *Journal of Financial Economics, 37*, 39–68.

Berle, A. & Means, G. (1932) *The Modern Corporation and Private Property.* New York.

Bettis, R.A. (1981) Performance differences in related and unrelated diversified firms. *Strategic Management Journal, 2*, 379–393.

Bettis, R.A. & Hall, W. K. (1982) Diversification strategy, accounting determined risks and accounting determined return. *Academy of Management Journal, 25*(2), 254–264.

Bradley, J. W. & Korn, D. H. (1981) *Acquisitions and Corporate Development.* Lexington.

Bressmer, C., Moser, A. C. & Sertl, W. (1989) *Vorbereitung und Abwicklung der Übernahme von Unternehmen.* Stuttgart, Berlin, Köln, Mainz.

Brudney, V. (1982) The Independent Director – Heavenly City or Potemkin Village? *Harvard Law Review, 95*, 597–659.

Bühner, R. (1990) *Erfolg von Unternehmenszusammenschlüssen in der Bundesrepublik Deutschland.* Stuttgart.

Bühner, R. (1991) *Grenzüberschreitende Zusammenschlüsse deutscher Unternehmen.* Stuttgart.

Cadbury, A. (1992) *Report of the Committee on the Financial Aspects of Corporate Governance,* London.

Cannella, A.A. & Hambrick, D.C. (1993) Effects of Executive Departures on the Performance of Acquired Firms. *Strategic Management Journal, 14,* 137–152.

Capron, L., Mitchell, W. & Swaminathan, A. (2001) Asset Divestiture Following Horizontal Acquisitions: A Dynamic View. *Strategic Management Journal, 22,* 817- 844.

Carpenter, M. *A.,* & Westphal, J. D. (2001) The Strategic Context of External Network Ties: Examining the Impact of Director Appointments on Board Involvement in Strategic Decision Making. *Academy of Management Journal, 44*(4), 639–660.

Cartwright, S. & Cooper, C.L. (1992) *Mergers and Acquisitions: The Human Factor.* Oxford.

Chatterjee, S., Lubatkin, M.H., Schweiger, D.M. & Weber, Y. (1992) Cultural Differences and Shareholder Value in Related Mergers: Linking Equity and Human Capital. *Strategic Management Journal, 13,* 319–334.

Coenenberg, A.G. & Sautter, M.T. (1988) Strategische und finanzielle Bewertung von Unternehmensakquisitionen. *Die Betriebswirtschaft, 48,* 691–710.

Comment, R. & Jarell, G. (1995) Corporate Focus and Stock Returns. *Journal of Financial Economics, 37,* 67–87.

Conyon, M.J., Grima, S., Thompson, S. & Wright, P.W. (2001) Do Hostile Mergers Destroy Jobs? *Journal of Economic Behavior and Organization, 45,* 427–440.

Daily, C.M., Dalton, D.R. & Cannella, A. A. (2003) Corporate Governance: Decades of Dialogue and Data. *Academy of Management Review, 28* (3), 371–382.

Dalton, D.R., Daily, C.M., Johnson, J. L. & Ellstrand, A.E. (1998) Meta-Analytic Reviews of Board Composition, Leadership Structure, and Financial Performance. *Strategic Management Journal, 19(3),* 269–290.

Dalton, D.R., Daily, C.M., Johnson, J. L. & Ellstrand, A.E. (1999) Number of Directors and Financial Performance: A Meta-Analysis. *Academy of Management Journal, 42*(6), 674–686.

Datta, D.K. (1991) Organizational Fit and Acquisition Performance: Effects of Post-Acquisition Integration. *Strategic Management Journal, 12,* 281–297.

Datta, D.K., Pinches, G.E. & Narayanan, V.K. (1992) ›Factors Influencing Wealth Creation from Mergers and Acquisitions: A Meta-analysis‹, *Strategic Management Journal,* 13, 67–84.

Davidson, W. N., Pilger, T. & Szakmary, A. (2004) The Importance of Board Composition and Committee Structure: The Case of Poison Pills. *Corporate Ownership & Control, 1*(3), 81–95.

Davis, JR. II., Schoorman, F. D. & Donaldson, L. (1997) Toward a Stewardship Theory of Management. *Academy of Management Review, 22*(1), 20–47.

Doukas, J. & Travlos, N.G. (1988) The Effect of Corporate Multinationalism on Shareholder's Wealth: Evidence from International Acquisitions. *The Journal of Finance, 43*, 1161–1175.

Drucker, P. (1974) *Management. Tasks, Responsibilities, Practices*. London.

Drucker, P. (1981) The five rules of successful acquisition. *The Wall Street Journal*, Thursday 15 October, 1981.

Drucker, P. (1991) *The New Society*. London. (Originalwerk publiziert 1950).

Drucker, P. (1993) *The New Society*. New York 1950. New edition, New Brunswick & London 1993.

Drucker, P. (1993) *The Practice of Management*. Reprinted paperback edition, Oxford.

Drucker P. (2004) *The Daily Drucker: 366 Days of Insight and Motivation for Getting the Right Things Done*. New York.

ECCH (2004) *Nestlé in 2004*, ICFAI Knowledge Center, Hyderabad, India.

Economiesuisse (2002) *Swiss Code of Best Practice for Corporate Governance*. Retrieved February 10, 2005, from www.economiesuisse.ch

Eisenhardt, K. & Bourgeois, L.J. (1988) Politics of Strategic Decision Making in High-Velocity Environments: A Midrange Theory. *Academy of Management Journal, 31*, 737–770.

Eisenhardt, K. (1989), Building theories from case research, *Academy of Management Review*, 14(4), 532–550.

Elsner, D.W. (1986) Risiken bei Unternehmensübernahmen in den USA. *Zeitschrift für betriebswirtschaftliche Forschung, 38*, 317–335.

E&Y (2003/1) Teil 1 Hunter Strategie, E&Y Bericht, Swissair, Detailbericht, Band 2.2.

E&Y (2003/2) Teil 2 Akquisition Flugbetriebe, E&Y Bericht, Swissair, Detailbericht, Band 2.2.

E&Y (2003/3) Teil 3 Akquisition flugnaher Betriebe, E&Y Bericht, Swissair, Detailbericht, Band 2.2.

E&Y (2003/4) Teil A Strategien und Strukturen der SairGroup, E&Y Bericht, Swissair, Untersuchungsergebnisse, Band 1.

Fama, E. & Jensen, M. (1983) Separation of Ownership and Control. *Journal of Law and Economics, 88*, 279–296.

Farschtschian, F. (2004) *Closing the Funding Gap*. Doctoral Seminar University of St.Gallen, 2004.

Finkelstein, S. & Hambrick, D. (1987) Managerial Discretion: A bridge between polar views on organizations. In L. Cummings & B. Staw (Eds.), *Research in Organizational Behavior, 9*, (pp. 369–406).

Finkelstein, S. & Hambrick, D. (1990) Top-Management-Team Tenure and Organizational Outcomes: The Moderating Role of Managerial Discretion. *Administrative Science Quarterly, 35*, 448–503.

Finkelstein, S. & Mooney, A. C. (2003) Not the Usual Suspects: How to Use Board Process to Make Boards Better. *Academy of Management Executive, 17*(2), 101–113.

Forbes, D. P. & Milliken, F.I. (1999). Cognition and Corporate Governance: Understanding Boards of Directors as Strategic Decision-Making Groups. *Academy of Management Review, 24*(3), 489–505.

Forstmoser, P. (1996) *Schweizerisches Aktienrecht.* Bern.

Fowler, K.L. & Schmidt, D.R. (1989) Determinants of Tender Offer Post-Acquisition Financial Performance. *Strategic Management Journal,* 10, 339–350.

Freeman, R.E. (1984) *Strategic Management: A Stakeholder Approach.* Boston.

Gaughan, P. A. (2007) *M&A and Corporate Restructurings,*.J.

Gerpott, T. J. (1993) *Integrationsgestaltung und Erfolg von Unternehmensakquisitionen,* Stuttgart.

Gertsen, M.C., Soderberg, A.M. & Torp, J.E. (1998) *Different Approaches to the Understanding of Culture in Mergers and Acquisitions.* In: M.C. Gertsen, A.M. Soderberg, & J.E. Torp, J.E. (Eds.), *deGruyter Studies in Organizations, Bd. 85: International Management, Organization and Policy Analysis* (pp. 17–38). Berlin, New York.

Ghoshal, S. & Haspeslagh, P. (1990) The Acquisition and Integration of Zanussi by Electrolux. *European Management Journal,* 8(4), 414–433.

Gilbert, M. Ruigrok, W. and Wicki, B. (2008) Research notes and commentaries: What passes as a rigorous case study? *Strategic Management Journal,* 29, 1465–1474.

Golden, B. & Zajac, E. (2001) *When* will boards influence strategy? Inclination x Power = Strategic change. *Strategic Management Journal, 22*(12), 1087–1111.

Gort, M. (1969) An economic disturbance theory of mergers. *Quarterly Journal of Economics, 83,* 624–64.

Hambrick, D. & Mason, P. (1984) Upper Echelons: The Organization as a Reflection of its Top Managers. *Academy of Management Review, 9,* 193–206.

Hambrick, D., Seung, C.T. & Chen, M.J. (1996) The Influence of Top Management Team Heterogeneity on Firms' Competitive Moves. *Administrative Science Quarterly, 41,* 659–684.

Hart, O. (1995) Corporate Governance: Some Theory and Implications. *The Economic Journal,* 105, 678–689.

Haspeslagh, P. C. & Jemison, D. B. (1991) *Managing Acquisitions: Creating Value through Corporate Renewal,* New York.

Hayward, M.L.A. & Hambrick, D.C. (1997) Explaining the Premiums Paid for Large Acquisitions: Evidence of CEO Hubris. *Administrative Science Quarterly, 42,* 103–127.

Heidrick & Struggles. (2003) *Is your Board fit for the Global Challenge? Corporate Governance in Europe.* Retrieved September 29, 2004, from www.heidrick.com

Henderson, B. (1979) *Henderson on Corporate Strategy.* Cambridge.

Hermalin, B. & Weisbach, M. (2001) *Boards of Directors as an Endogenously Determined Institution: A Survey of the Economic Literature.* NBER Working Paper no. W8161.

Heriott, R., Firestone W. (1983) Multisite qualitative policy research: Optimizing description and generalizability. *Educational Researcher,* 12, 14–19.

Hilb, M. (2002) *Transnationales Management der Human-Ressourcen. Das 4-P Modell des Glocalpreneuring*. Neuwied.

Hilb, M. (2002) *Inegrated Board Management in International Companies*, 2002, University of St. Gallen.

Hilb, M. (2004) Strategic and Integrated Board Management. St. Gallen, Doctoral Seminar Papter, Summer Semester 2004.

Hilb, M. (2005) *New Corporate Governance*. Heidelberg.

Hiliman, A. T. & Dalziel, T. (2003) Boards of Directors and Finn Performance: Integrating Agency and Resource Dependence Perspectives. *Academy of Management Review, 28*(3), 383–396.

Hilmer, F. G. & the Independent Working Party into Corporate Governance (1993) *Strictly Boardroom: Improving Governance to Enhance Company Performance*. Melbourne.

Hitt, M., Hoskisson, R. & Kim, H. (1997) International Diversification: Effects on Innovation and Firm Performance in Product-diversified Firms. *Academy of Management Journal, 40*, 767–798.

Hofstede, G. (1980) *Culture's Consequences: International Difference in Work Related Values*. Beverly Hills.

Hughes, A., Mueller, D. C. & Singh, A. (1980) Hypothesis about Mergers. In D. C. Mueller (Ed.), *The Determinants and Effects of Mergers. An International Comparison*. Cambridge.

Humpert, F.W. (1992) Unternehmensakquisitionen – Erfahrungen beim Kauf von Unternehmen. In: W. Busse v. Colbe, A. & G. Coenenberg (Hrsg.), *Unternehmensakquisition und Unternehmensbewertung* (S. 357–373). Stuttgart.

Huse, M. (2005) Accountability and Creating Accountability: A Framework for Exploring Behavioural Perspectives of Corporate Governance. *British Journal of Management, 16*, 65.

Hyland, M.M. & Marcellino, P.A. (2002) Examining Gender on Corporate Boards: A Regional Study. *Corporate Governance: The International Journal of Effective Board Performance, 2*(4), 24–31.

IHT (2007) Swissair executives assert innocence at first day of Switzerland's biggest corporate trial, *International Herald Tribune*, 15.12007.

Insite (2010) Independent Firms To Dominate M&A Scene in 2010. By Stacy Schultz, Financial Planning. 8 January 2010. available at www.financial-planning.com

Jarillo, J.C. (2003) *Strategic Logic*. New York.

Jemison, D.B. & Sitkin, S.B. (1986) Corporate Acquisitions: A process perspective. *Academy of Management Review 11*(1), 145–163.

Jensen, M. C. (1984) Takeovers: Folklore and science. *Harvard Business Review, 62*(6), 109–121.

Jensen, M.C. (1986) Agency Costs of Free Cash Flow, Corporate Finance, and Takeovers. *American Economic Review, 76*, 323–329.

Jensen, M. C. (1986) The takeover controversy: Analysis and evidence. *Midland Corporate Finance Journal, 4*(2), 6–27.

Jensen, M. & Meckling, W. (1976) Theory of the Firm: Managerial Behaviour, Agency Cost, and Ownership Structure. *Journal of Financial Economics, 3*, 305–360.

Jensen, M.C. & Ruback, R.S. (1983) The market for corporate control: The scientific evidence. *Journal of Financial Economics, 11*, 5–50.

Judge, W. & Zeithaml, C. (1990) *An Empirical Examination of the Board's Involvement in the Strategic Decision Making Process.* Paper presented at the Academy of Management Meeting.

Keller, H.U. (2003) *The Determinants and Effects on Interlocking Directorships and Board Composition: An Empirical Analysis of Corporate Governance in Switzerland.* Unpublished Dissertation, University of St. Gallen, St. Gallen.

Kesner, I. F. (1988) Directors' Characteristics and Committee Membership: An Investigation of Type, Occupation, Tenure, and Gender. *Academy of Management Journal, 31*(1), 66–84.

King, D. R., Dalton, D. R., Daily C. M. & Covin, J. G. (2004). Meta-analysis of postacquisition performance: Indications of unidentified moderators. *Strategic Management Journal, 25*(2), 187–200.

Kitching, J. (1973) Acquisitions in Europe, Causes of Corporate Successes and Failures. *Business International, 2*, 20–35.

Klein, A. (1998) Firm Performance and Board Committee Structure. *Journal of Law & Economics, 41*(1), 275–303.

Kogut, B. & Zander, U. (1996) What firms do? Coordination, Identity, and Learning. *Organization Science, 7*, 502–518.

Kootz, E. (1996) *Structural holes, market constraints, and embedding strategies: an empirical analysis of mergers & acquisitions in Germany.* Hallstadt.

Kusewitt, J.B. (1985) An Exploratory Study of Acquisition Factors Relating to Performance. *Strategic Management Journal, 6*, 151–169.

Krystek, U. (1992) Unternehmenskultur und Akquisition. *Zeitschrift für Betriebswirtschaft, 62*, 539–565.

Lambrecht, B. & and Stewar M. (2007) A Theory of Takeovers and Disinvestment, *Journal of Finance 62*, 809–845.

Lang, L.H.P. & Stulz, R.M. (1994) Tobin's Q, Corporate Diversification and Firm Performance. *Journal of Political Economy, 102*, 1248–1280.

Lawrence, B. S. (1997) The Black Box of Organizational Demography. *Organization Science, 8*(1), 1–22.

Leonard-Barton, D. (1990) A dual methodology for case studies: Synergistic use of a longitudinal single site with replicated multiple sites. *Organization Science* 1(3), 248–266.

Lorsch, T. W. & MacIver, E. (1989) *Pawns or Potentates: The Reality of America's Corporate Boards.* Boston.

Lubatkin, M. & O'Neill, H.M. (1987) Merger Strategies and Capital Market Risk. *American Management Journal, 30*, 665–684.

Luechinger, R. (2001) *Der Fall der Swissair.* Zuerich.

Macharzina, K. & Wolf, J. (2005) *Unternehmensführung: das internationale Managementwissen: Konzepte – Methoden – Praxis.* Wiesbaden.

Mace, M.L.G. (1971) *Directors: Myth and Reality*. Boston: Division of Research Graduate School of Business Administration Harvard University.

Macus, M. (2002) *Towards a comprehensive and dynamic perspective on boards: Theory development and conceptual development*. In Doctoral Thesis Nr. 2677. Bamberg.

Macus, M. (2003) *Towards a Comprehensive Theory of Boards*. Dissertation, University of St. Gallen, St. Gallen.

Makadok, R. (2001) Towards a Synthesis of the Resource-Based and Dynamic Capability Views of Rent Creation. *Strategic Management Journal, 22*, 387–401.

Malik, F. (1999) Anforderungen an die Unternehmungsführung. In H. Siegwart, G. & G. Negebauer G (Hrsg.), *Mega-Fusionen, Analysed-Kontroversen, Perspektiven* (2. Aufl.). Bern.

Malik, F. (2001) Kardinalfehler in der Swissair Strategie, in *Neue Zürcher Zeitung*, 25.7.2001.

Malik, F. (2002) *Die Neue Corporate Governance*. Frankfurt am Main.

Malik, F. (2002) *Die Neue Corporate Governance*. 3. Aufl., Frankfurt am Main, p 26 ff.

Malik, F.(2003) Fragen und Antworten. *malik on management – m.o.m. letter*, März 2003.

Malik, F. (2007) *Management: Das A und O des Handwerks*. Frankfurt am Main.

Malik, F. (2008) *Unternehmenspolitik und Corporate Governance*. Frankfurt am Main.

Manne, H. G. (1965) Mergers and the market for corporate control. *Journal of Political Economy, 73*, 110–120.

Marris, R. (1963) A Model of the »Managerial« Enterprise. *Quarterly Journal of Economics, 77*, 185–209.

Maucher, H. (1992) ›*Marketing ist Chefsache*‹,.Berlin

Maucher, H. (2007) ›*Management Breviary: A Guideline to Corporate Success*‹. Frankfurt am Main.

McCann, J. E. & Gilkey, R. (1988) *Joining Forces, Creating and Managing Successful Mergers and Acquisitions*. Englewood Cliffs, NJ.

Minichilli, A. & Hansen, C. (2004) *The Board Roles Involvement at Different Life Cycle Stages*. A *Contingency Perspective*. Paper presented at the EURAM, SI. Andrews. May 5–8, 2004.

Milgrom, P. & Roberts, J. (1995) Complementarities and Fit: Strategy, Structure, and Organizational Change in Manufacturing. *Journal of Accounting and Economics, 19*, 179–205.

Milliken, F.J. & Martins, L.L. (1996) Searching for Common Threads: Understanding the Multiple Effects of Diversity in Organizational Groups. *Academy of Management Review, 21(2), 402–433*.

Mintzberg, H. (1983) *Power In and Around Organizations*. Englewood Cliffs, NJ.

Mintzberg, H., Raisinghani, D. & Andre, T. (1976) The Structure of »Unstructured« Decision Processes. *Administrative Science Quarterly, 21*, 246–275.

Mizruchi, M.S. (1996) What do Interlocks Do? An Analysis, Critique, and Assessment of Research on Interlocking Directories. *Annual Review of Sociology, 22*(1), 271–287.

Monks, R. & Minow, N. (2001) *Corporate Governance* (2nd ed.). Oxford.

Morck, R., Shleifer, A. & Vishny, R.W. (1990) Do Managerial Objectives Drive Bad Acquisitions? *Journal of Finance, 45,* 31–48.

Mueller, D.C. (1980) *The Determinants and Effects of Mergers: An International Comparison.* Cambridge.

Mueller, D.C. (1987) The Corporation: Growth, Diversification and Mergers. In A. Jacquemin (Hrsg.), *Theory of the Firm and Industrial Organization,* Chur et al.

Murray, A. (1989) Top Management Group Heterogeneity and Firm Performance. *Strategic Management Journal, 10,* 125–141.

Nahavandi, A. & Malekzadeh, P. (1988) Acculturation in Mergers and Acquisitions. *Academy of Management Review, 13,* 79–90.

Naman, J.L. & Slevin, D.P. (1993) Entrepreneurship and the Concept of Fit: A Model and Empirical Tests. *Strategic Management Journal, 14,* 137–153.

Neary, J. (2007) Empirical research on the resource-based view of the firm: an assessment and suggestions for future research. *Strategic Management Jornal, Vol.28, No.2,* 121–146.

Nelson, R.R. & Winter, S.G. (1982) *An Evolutionary Theory of Economic Change.* Cambridge.

NZZ (1998) Honegger als Swissair Group Präsident nominiert, *Neue Zürcher Zeitung.* 8.10.1998.

NZZ (2001/1) Rücktritt Philippe Bruggisser, *Neue Zürcher Zeitung.* 24.1.2001.

NZZ (2001/2) Wir stehen zu unserer Verantwortung, *Neue Zürcher Zeitung,* 10.3.2001.

NZZ (2001/3) Nicht durchwegs schlüssige Swissair Bilanzen, *Neue Zürcher Zeitung* 16.3.2001.

NZZ (2001/4) Keine Schwachstellen?, *Neue Zürcher Zeitung.* 16.3.2001.

NZZ (2001/5) Kühles Agieren Cortis, *Neue Zürcher Zeitung.* 3.4.2001.

NZZ (2001/6) Das Fiasko der Swissair in der Retrospektive, *Neue Zürcher Zeitung.* 23.4.2001.

NZZ (2001/7) Das Debakel, *Neue Zürcher Zeitung.* 3.10.2001.

NZZ (2001/8) Nationale Fluggesellschaften – eine Realität, *Neue Zürcher Zeitung.* 7.11.2001.

NZZ (2002) Wann wird aus Networking *Filz, Neue Zürcher Zeitung.* 23.11.2002.

Oliver, R.W. (2000) The Board's Role: Driver's Seat or Rubber Stamp? *Journal of Business Strategy, 21*(4), 7–9.

O'Neal, D. & Thomas, H. (1996) Developing the Strategic Board. *Long Range Planning, 29*(3), 314–327.

Paine, F.T. & Power, D.J. Merger Strategy: An Examination of Drucker's Five Rules for Successful Acquisitions. *Strategic Management Journal, 5,* 99–110.

Pearce, J.A. II & Zahra, S.A. (1991) The Relative Power of CEOs and Boards of Directors: Associations with Corporate Performance. *Strategic Management Journal, 12,* 135–153.

Peteraf, M.A. (1993) The Cornerstones of Competitive Advantage: A Resource Based View. *Strategic Management Journal, 14,* 179–191.

Pettigrew, A. (1992) On Studying Managerial Elites. *Strategic Management Journal,* 13(8), 163–182.

Pfeffer, J. (1972) Size and Composition of Corporate Board of Directors: The Organization and Its Environment. *Administrative Science Quarterly,* 7, 218–229.

Pfeffer, J. & Salancik, G.R. (1978) *The External Control of Organizations: A Resource Dependence Perspective.* New York.

Porter, M. (1980) *Competitive Strategy.* New York.

Porter, M. (1987) From Competitive Advantage to Corporate Strategy. *Harvard Business Review,* 65, 43–59.

Prahalad, C.K. & Hamel, G. (1990) The Core Competence of the Corporation. *Harvard Business Review,* 68, 79–91.

Probst, G., Mecier, J. (1992) *Observing Swissair's Culture.* Discussion Paper 11, Université de Genève, Genève.

Provan, J. (1980) Board Power and Organizational Effectiveness Among Human Service Agencies. *Academy of Management Journal,* 23, 221–236.

Puempin, C. (1990) *Meilensteine im Management.* Basel.

Rappaport, A. (1998) *Creating Shareholder Value* (2nd ed.). New York.

Ravenscraft, D.J. (1987) The 1980's merger wave: An industrial organization perspective. In L.E. Browne & E.S. Rosengren (Eds.), *The Merger Boom* (pp.17–37). Boston.

Ravenscraft, D.J. & Scherer, F.M. (1987a) Life after takeover. *The Journal of Industrial Economics,* 16(2), 147–156.

Ravenscraft, D.J. & Scherer, F.M. (1987b) *Merger, Sell-Offs, and Economic Efficiency.* Washington D.C.

Rhoades, D.L., Rechner, P.L. & Sundaramurthy, C. (2000). Board Composition and Financial Performance: A Meta-Analysis of the Influence of Outside Directors. *Journal of Managerial Issues,* 12(1), 76–91.

Richard, O. & Shelor, R. (2002) Linking top management team age heterogeneity to firm performance: juxtaposing two mid-range theories. *The International Journal of Human Resource Management,* 13, 958–974.

Roberts, J., McNulty, T. & Stiles, P. (2005) Beyond Agency Conceptions of the Work of the Non-Executive Directors: Creating Accountability in the Boardroom. *British Journal of Management,* 16(1), 5–26.

Roll, R. (1986) The hubris hypothesis of corporate takeovers. *Journal of Business,* 59, 197–216.

Rosenstein, J. (1987) Why Don't U.S. Boards Get More Involved in Strategy? *Long Range Planning,* 20, 20–34.

Rumelt, R.P. (1974) *Strategy, Structure and Economic Performance,* Cambridge.

Rumelt, R.P. (1982) Diversification Strategy and Profitability. *Strategic Management Journal,* 3, 359–369.

Ruigrok, W., Peck, S. & Van del' Linde, C. (2004) *Strange Bedfellows: Foreigners on Top Management Teams and Boards.* Unpublished manuscript, St. Gallen.

Salter, M. & Weinhold, W. (1982) What lies ahead for merger activities in the 1980s. *Journal of Business Strategy,* 2(4), 66–99.

Sanders, W.M.G. & Carpenter, M.A. (1998) Internationalization and Firm Governance: The Roles of CEO Compensation, Top Team Composition, and Board Structure. *Academy of Management Journal, 41(2),* 158–178.

Scherer, F.M. & Ross D. (1990) *Industrial Market Structure and Economic Performance.* Boston.

Schmidt, D.R. & Fowler, K.L. (1990) Post-acquisition Financial Performance and Executive Compensation. *Strategic Management Journal,* 11, 559–569.

Schumpeter, J.A. (1942) *Capitalism, Socialism and Democracy.* New York.

Shleifer, A. & Vishny, R. (1997) A Survey of Corporate Governance. *Journal of Finance, 52* (2), 737–783.

Singh, H. & Montgomery, C. (1987) Corporate Acquisition Strategies and Economic Performance. *Strategic Management Journal,* 8, 377–386.

Smith, A. (1776) *An Inquiry into the Nature and Causes of the Wealth of Nations.* Online publication. Available at www.econlib.org

Smith, K.G., Smith K.A., Olian, D., Sims, H.P., O'Bannon, D. & Scully, J.A. (1994) Top Management Team Demography and Process: The Role of Social Integration and Communication. *Administrative Science Quarterly, 39,* 412–438.

Steiner, P.O. (1975) *Mergers: Motives, Effects, Politics.* Ann Arbor.

Stiles, P. & Taylor, B. (2001) *Boards at Work: How Directors View their Roles and Responsibilities.* Oxford.

Straub, T. (2006) *Reasons for Frequent Failure in Mergers and Acquisitions, A Comprehensive Analysis.* Wiesbaden.

Swissair (1992) Annual-Report, 1991, Zuerich, Swissair.

Swissair (1994) Annual Report, 1993, Zuerich, Swissair.

Swissair (1995) Annual Report, 1994, Zuerich: Swissair.

Swissair (1996) Annual Report, 1995, Zuerich: Swissair.

Swissair (1997) Annual Report, 1996, Zuerich: Swissair.

Swissair (1999) Annual Report, 1998, Zuerich: Swissair.

Swissair (2000) Annual Report, 1999, Zuerich, Swissair.

Swissair (2001) Annual Report, 2000, Zuerich: Swissair.

SWX. (2002) *Directive on Information Relating to Corporate Governance.* Retrieved January 10, 2005, from www.swx.com

Tashakori, A. & Boulton, W. (1985) A Look At the Board's Role in Planning. *The Journal of Business Strategy, 3,* 64–70.

Teece, D.J. (1987) Profiting from Technological Innovation: Implications for Integration, Collaboration, Licensing and Public Policy. In D.J. Teece, D.J. (Ed.), *The Competitive Challenge. Strategies for Industrial Innovation and Renewal* (pp. 185–219). New York.

Third Way for Germany (2005, 6. Februar) *Business Week.*

Trautwein, F. (1990) Merger Motives and Merger Prescriptions. *Strategic Management Journal, 11,* 283–295.

Tricker, R. I. (1984) *Corporate Governance: Practices, Procedures, and Powers in British Companies and their Boards of Directors.* Aldershot.

UNCATD (2000) *Cross-border mergers and acquisitions. World Investment Report.* New York.

UNCTAD. (2002) *World Investment Report 2002.* Transnational Corporations and Export Competitiveness. New York; Geneva.

Vaara, E. (1993) *Finnish-Swedish Mergers and Acquisitions: An Empirical Analysis of Success,* Helsinki University of Technology, Industrial Economics and Industrial Psychology, Report No. 147. Otaniemi.

Vafeas, N. (2003) Length of Board Tenure and Outside Director Independence. *Journal of Business Finance* & *Accounting, 30*(7/8), 1043–1064.

Vance, S. C. (1983) *Corporate Leadership: Boards, Directors, and Strategy.* New York.

Van Hamel, J. A., van Wijk, R E., de Rooij, A. J. R, & Bruel, M. (1998) Boardroom Dynamics – Lessons in Governance. *Corporate Governance: An International Review, 6* (3), 193–201.

Venkatraman, N. & Camillus, J.C. (1984) Exploring the Concept of »Fit« in Strategic Management. *Academy of Management Review, 9,* 513–525.

Vermeulen, F. & Barkema, H. (2001) Learning Through Acquisitions. *Academy of Management Journal, 44,* 457–476.

Very, P., Lubatkin, M., Calori, R. & Veiga, J. (1997) Relative Standing and the Performance of Recent European Mergers. *Strategic Management Journal, 18,* 593-615.

Walsh, J.P. & Seward, J.K. (1990) On the efficiency of internal and external corporate control mechanisms. *Academy of Management Review, 15,* 421–458.

Weber, Y., Shenkar, O. & Raveh, A. (1996) National versus Corporate Cultural Fit in Mergers and Acquisitions: An Exploratory Study. *Management Science, 42,* 1215–1227.

Wernerfelt, B. (1984) A Resource-based View of the Firm. *Strategic Management Journal, 5,* 171–180.

Wiersema, M. & Bantel, K. (1992) Top Management Team Demography and Corporate Strategic Change. *Academy of Management Journal, 35,* 91–121.

Williamson, O. (1984) Corporate Governance. *Yale Law Journal, 93,* 1197–1230.

Williamson, O. (1985) Employee Ownership and Internal Governance. *Journal of Economic Behaviour and Organization, 6,* 243–245.

Yin, R. (1994) *Case Study Research: Design and Methods.* London.

Yin, R (2009) *Case Study Research: Design and Methods.* New York.

Zahra, S. & Pearce, J. (1989) Boards of Directors and Corporate Financial Performance: A Review and Integrative Model. *Journal of Management,* 15, 291–344.

Zahra, S. & Pearce, J. (1992) ›Board Composition from a Strategic Contingency Perspective‹, *Journal of Management Studies, 29,* 411–438.

Zahra, S. & Schulte, W. (1992) ›Four Modes of Board of Directors' Participation in Corporate Strategy‹, *American Business Review, 10(1),* 78–87.

Index